D0223086

The Other Indians:

A Political And Cultural History

of South Asians In America

Vinay Lal

Asian American Studies Center Press
University Of California, Los Angeles

2008

ISBN 978-0-934052-41-7

CO-EDITORS: Russell C. Leong and Don T. Nakanishi

COPYEDITOR: Stephanie D. Santos

GRAPHIC DESIGN/PRODUCTION COORDINATOR: Mary Uyematsu Kao

All photographs and images in this publication
are courtesy of Vinay Lal and Stephanie D. Santos

Cover photographs—

Frontcover: Vinay Lal   Indian Student Union, Annual Culture
Show, University of California, Los Angeles, May 2005.

Backcover: Stephanie D. Santos

UCLA Asian American Studies Center Press
3230 Campbell Hall, Box 951546
Los Angeles, CA 90095-1546
http://www.aasc.ucla.edu
Telephone: (310) 825-2968; FAX (310) 206-9844
Email: aascpress@aasc.ucla.edu

Printed in the United States of America.

Gandhi's Talisman, Mantra for a Free World.

Photographs: Vinay Lal, 2006.

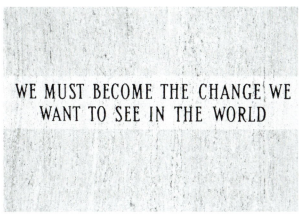

Inscription on a statue of Mohandas Gandhi, Skokie, Illinois.

Mural in a Chicago Park.

to the memory of two
talented and beautiful friends
dreamers both
perhaps sensitive to a fault
who departed early
from this world

Mahadai Das (Guyana 1954 – Guyana 2003, via the U.S.)
philosopher, activist,
rebel and beauty queen,
poetess of her people

They came in ships.

From across the seas, they came.
Britain, colonising India, transporting her chains

from Chota Nagpur and the Ganges Plain.

Westwards came the Whitby,
The Hesperus,
The Island-bound Fatel Rozack.

Wooden missions of imperialist design.

and

Reetika Vazirani (India 1962 – U.S. 2003)
poet, writer, critic
voice of the diaspora

Culture shock is not your reflex upon leaving
                                        the dock;
it is when you have been a law-abiding citizen
for more than ten years: when someone asks
                                        your name
and the name of your religion and your first thought is
I don't know, or you can't remember what you said
                                        last time;
you think there is something you forgot to sign:
your oath, for one; and you are positive
those green-shirted workmen in the room right now
want to take you in for questioning.

TABLE OF CONTENTS

ACKNOWLEDGEMENTS

I am grateful to Don Nakanishi and Russell Leong, both for entrusting the inaugural volume of this UCLA Asian American Studies Center monograph series, "Professor in a Pocket," to me, and for their close reading of the entire manuscript. I am similarly thankful to Daniel M. Neuman for his suggestions and editorial notes. Surendra Bhana went well beyond the call of duty in responding with alacrity to my request for a careful reading of the manuscript, and I am extremely grateful to him for his many thoughtful and learned suggestions, not all of which it was possible for me to accept, for improving the book. I would also like to thank the anonymous reviewer of the manuscript for the UCLA Asian American Studies Center Press.

The research for this book has been facilitated over the last few years by grants from the Academic Senate of the University of California, Los Angeles, and, in particular, the unstinting support of the Asian American Studies Center. Their assistance is gratefully acknowledged. I would also like to express my appreciation to the staff of the Asian American Studies Center, especially Mary Uyematsu Kao and Stephanie Santos, for their help in bringing this work to publication.

LIST OF PHOTOGRAPHS

INTRODUCTION:

The Politics of Identity and a Note on Usage

This is a book about the other Indians—the Indians other than those who once vastly populated the Americas, experiencing a calamitous decline in their numbers after their encounter with representatives of the enlightened West. The indigenous inhabitants of the Americas have, when viewed as a collectivity, been known by a plethora of names, among them Amerindians, American Indians, native Americans, and most simply as Indians. By whatever name these Indians are known, they seemingly do not have much of a shared history with the Indians, the subject of this book, who arrived in the Americas from Asia or the Indian subcontinent. And yet, their histories are inextricably intertwined, for much more than the obvious reason that, at least in the United States, American Indians and South Asian Indians have sometimes been confused for each other. Vasco da Gama was to arrive in India only a few years after Columbus, who imagined he had reached India, set landfall in the Americas. Much has mistakenly been made of Columbus's mistake, since in the age of European exploration, expansion, and conquest there were bound to be few survivors of the onslaught by colonizers who acted with singular determination and self-aggrandizement in their quest for riches and domination. The colonizers stumbled upon some outsiders, deliberately set themselves upon others, and targeted yet others for chastisement—everywhere they unleashed a regime of oppression. The outcome, however, was not the same in every respect. A few Indian commentators have of late been speaking with enthusiasm of the reverse colonization of Britain. At the other extreme, however much Indian Americans may complain of not being given due recognition, American Indians are unquestionably the most tragic instantiation of the invisible minority in the U.S. Ironically, Indian Americans, whose share of the U.S. population matches that of American Indians, are now set to outstrip the latter. It is a cruel twist of fate that one group of Indians has, in a manner of speaking, had to become nearly redundant to pave the way for another. This is as painful a fact as any for Indian Americans.

Much like American Indians, Indian Americans are known by many other designations, none of which has universal acceptance among Indian Americans themselves. The scholarly and popular literature also reference them as Asian Indians, South Asians, South Asian Americans, and *desis*, though as the early chapters of this book suggest, there have been other designations that were once in vogue, among them Aryans, Caucasians, and even "Hindoos" to characterize all people coming from what was then British India. Advocates of Hindu nationalism in the United States have in recent years been championing the word "Bharatiyas," or people who derive their origin from "Bharat," the official name for India that appears on the country's postage stamps, coins, and official documents. At the other end of the political spectrum, many progressive activists have opted for the word "desi," or those who are, so to speak, of the "desh" (of one's own country). Those who are of the desh are not from *videsh* (a foreign land). This opposition perhaps received its fullest expression in the nationalist period, though one should not think that all advocates of *swadeshi*—pertaining to one's own country—or of *swaraj* (self determination; self-rule, but equally rule over one's own self) had the most unedifying and jingoistic conceptions of nationalism in mind.

Though there is no gainsaying the fact that many proponents of the term "desi" similarly seek to invoke its widest and most pluralistic meanings, calling forth the shared lives of many South Asians, the term operates on many different and disjunctive registers. As I have often been reminded by an old friend from Jaisalmer, in western Rajasthan, words such as "country" mean quite different things to people from metropolitan centers and those who earn their livelihoods in India's tens of thousands of villages and smaller towns.   When my friend chances to remark,"*Hamare desh me aisa hota hai*" ("This is how it happens in our country"), by *desh* he clearly means his part of the country.   The observation invokes not so much the nation in the abstract, much less Bharat, but rather a frame of mind and a set of habits.   The word "desi" also calls to mind home-grown products: thus, for example, now that liberalization has opened the Indian market to a whole array of foreign goods, including Western/hybrid varieties of fruits and vegetables, one hears often of the contrast between foreign vegetables and those branded "desi"—the latter being smaller and (in common belief) much more palatable to the taste than foreign varieties. There is, it appears to me, something unsettling and certainly odd about the fact that the most enthusiastic proponents of the word "desi" are precisely those diasporic Indians who, in many ways, have least claim to the word and its multiple inheritanc-es, considering their location in metropolitan centers of thought and their immense distance from local and vernacular knowl-edge systems.   For these reasons among many, I have, except in a few particular instances, eschewed the word "desi" when speaking of Indian Americans.

The term "Asian Indian" was introduced in the U.S. Census of 1980 and sets apart someone so designated from "American Indian." I have deployed this term on a few occasions when referring to what we might think of as the official or legisla-tive history of Indian Americans since 1980, but this term does not enjoy wide recognition among Indian Americans. What-ever the attachment of Asian Indians to India, or to particular aspects of the history and culture of India, they also like to think of themselves as Americans—and "Asian Indian" brings no fulfillment in this respect. To that extent, "Asian Indian" cannot be considered analogous to "American Indian." This leaves, for our consideration, the term "South Asian Ameri-cans." India has been a civilization much longer than it has been a nation-sate, and however different the paths taken by India, Pakistan, and Bangladesh in recent years, one recog-nizes that the subcontinent's contours have not been shaped exclusively or even predominantly by the ideology of the nation-state. The term "South Asia" serves, then, as a rebuke to those who are excessively bound by nationalist sentiments, or who otherwise conflate India with Hindu just as they have effortlessly come to the conclusion that Pakistan and Bangladesh can be tolerated by India but must never be allowed to achieve anything remotely resembling parity.

However, though there is undoubtedly a good case to be made for using the term "South Asian Americans", the difficulties in so doing cannot be minimized. In my experience, many Americans, academics not excepted, are likely to confuse South Asia with Southeast Asia, and the American experience of Vietnam has etched firmly into place a certain conception of that part of the world. But to come to more considerable problems: I find it a touch surprising that secular and progressive people who are most inclined to use the term, and whose anti-imperialism is also on record, are not much deterred by the fact that the term is essentially a creation of post-World War II American geopolitics. South Asian countries themselves have moved closer in recent years to embracing the idea of South Asia, as represented in such organizations as SAARC (South Asian Association for Regional Cooperation), but it is well to remember that South Asia is comprised not only of Pakistan, Bangladesh, and India, but also of Nepal, Sri Lanka, Bhutan, and the Maldives. Afghanistan was admitted to SAARC only in 2007, but is not typically viewed as falling under the orbit of South Asia. And what, one might ask, of the long ties of India with Burma (now Myanmar)? The arbitrariness of "South Asia" aside, I have not seen any substantive discussion of South Asians in the United States that offers an account of the history of Sri Lankans and Nepalese. To be sure, one can defend a more narrower conception of South Asia such that it would only encompass India, Pakistan, and Bangladesh—the three nation-states that eventually, following the liberation of East Pakistan in 1971, emerged from the partition of 1947—but I think all this should suffice to indicate why the idea of South Asia creates its own muddles.

While many progressive and secular organizations have come together on a common South Asian platform, I have encountered few very people in the wider Pakistani, Indian, and

Bangladeshi communities in the U.S. who are willing to embrace the term. The reticence of Indians, especially, in being marked "South Asian" is more pronounced in the aftermath of the September 11, 2001 bombings of the World Trade Center and the Pentagon, as well as the witch hunts that, around the world, have sent thousands of innocent Muslims to jail, pushed others into the commission of desperate acts, and cast a pall of suspicion around all Muslim males. A Sikh male was among the very first people killed in the U.S. in retaliation for the September 11 bombings. His only mistake was to sport a turban on his head, as do most Sikh men, and so open himself up to attack as a likely follower of Osama bin Laden. Not all Muslim men wear turbans, nor are all bearers of turbans Muslims: but such niceties matter not a jot to perpetrators of crime, whether found on streets or in the corridors of power. Discrimination against Muslim women workers and students wearing burqas and chadors has also been reported in the U.S. and elsewhere. There were other widely reported instances of violence against South Asians, and U.S. and state government agencies themselves issued alerts to the effect that men with origins from the Middle East or South Asia were especially vulnerable. To point out that there were no South Asian men among the criminals who fomented and executed the terrorist attacks is accurate, but any such assertion gives rise to what I would describe as "ethical awkwardness." Should one defend oneself with the perhaps implied proposition that the violence is more legitimately targeted elsewhere? Absolutely nothing can ever justify retaliatory violence that is predicated on the principle of collective or associative guilt.

Pakistan and Bangladesh are predominantly Muslim states, as India, notwithstanding its immense Muslim population, is not. This is a fact that weighs heavily on the minds of Indian Americans; it is also a consideration supreme in the minds of U.S. government officials, as the exemption of India, which has a substantially greater Muslim population than any country in the Middle East, from Special Registration amply illustrates. (This legislation, passed a few months after the September 11 bombings, required males resident in the U.S.—but not

U.S. citizens—and claiming nationality from a list of some thirty countries to register with Homeland Security.)   One might reasonably argue that ethical considerations and political solidarity demand that Indian Americans cast their lot with fellow South Asians in these difficult times. The only genuine test of humanity, more than one great reformer has argued, is to share the suffering of others. On the other hand, there is the brute fact that being identified as a Muslim brings one no rewards; indeed, even remote association with one triggers suspicious looks. One can understand why, from a purely pragmatic standpoint, Indian Americans might loathe being lumped as South Asians. We should perhaps look forward to the time when, in an act of Gandhian mass nonviolent resistance, all human beings take on the identity of those who are oppressed. What other dialectics of emancipation is at all possible?

I have, in conclusion, opted for the term "Indian American" above all its competitors. It appears to me to best do justice to those people who are the subject of this book. Their history is singular, as is the history of all other immigrant groups who have made their way to the United States; but, by the same token, it is not so singularly exceptional that Indians cannot take their place alongside Chinese Americans, Arab Americans, Korean Americans, African Americans, and many others. To say as much is to concede nothing at all to those historians and sociologists who believe that assimilation into American society should be the objective of every immigrant group. I have put on record here a very different interpretation of the history and culture of Indian Americans, but I shall leave it the reader to reach her or his own conclusions.

The Other Indians:

A Political And Cultural History

of South Asians In America

Indians in the Global Setting

The Indian diaspora today, more so than ever before, is an incontestable fact of world culture. Notwithstanding the debates that have animated the field of diaspora studies on the appositeness of the word "diaspora" to describe the dispersal of people such as the Chinese, Armenians, Indians, and Palestinians around the world, no one has found a better term to characterize the global presence of the Chinese or, to take another example, the Little Armenias that dot many landscapes. Should that single term, and no such term is ever without its politics, be allowed to illustrate both the dispersed history of the English people, whose presence can be found in Scotland, Ireland, South Africa, New Zealand, Canada, India, the United States, Australia, and elsewhere, as much as the contours of the bewildering global Indian diaspora, the history of which in part was shaped by the colonizing English who brought over indentured laborers to the Caribbean, Fiji, Mauritius, Malaysia, and South Africa? Perhaps the word "diaspora" flattens too much and fails to distinguish between diasporas of the colonized and of the colonizer, diasporas that have arisen under circumstances of extreme repression and diasporas that suggest more benign histories of ambition, self-improvement, economic advancement, or sheer adventure.

If diasporas are not equal and their political histories are writ large in the language of dominance and power, it is also instructive to remember that a global diaspora may itself be constituted of often vastly unequal parts. The colonizing diaspora of the English was comprised not only of Oxbridge graduates, planters, missionaries, and civil servants, but convicts and various classes of subalterns. And so to the question: what language best describes the history of some 15 million overseas Indians, or, in the language of the Indian government, "People of Indian Origin" (PIO)? If these are, to invoke another favored official term with a checkered history, "Non-Resident Indians," how should we characterize the millions of middle-class Indians who, though physically settled in Bangalore, Mumbai, or Delhi, are plotting futures in the United States of America or are already, in their gated American-style communities, living apart from the majority of Indians? Indeed, should one wish to write a history of the global Indian diaspora, it would become incumbent to ask just what is common, other than descent from some place imagined as India, to Indo-Trinidadians, British Gujaratis, Indo-Guyanese Americans, Punjabi Mexican Americans, Vancouver Sikhs, South African Indians, Creole-speaking Indo-Mauritians, and countless number of communities that may own up to some element of Indianness in their history or sense of self? One suspects that to write a history of the global Indian diaspora is to initiate an inquiry into "Indianness."

What is indubitably true is that the once largely forgotten history of the Indian diaspora, which encompasses diverse narratives of migration, displacement, homelessness, economic exchanges, cross-cultural transactions, hybrid literatures, and new identity formations, has now been woven into contemporary stories of globalization and transnational movements. South Asians have transformed the face of the country that once colonized them. To eat well in England, Somerset Maugham once wrote, one had to have an English breakfast three times a day, but Manchester's Curry Mile and the thousand-plus Indian restaurants in London alone have added much cheer to lifestyles previously hobbled by notorious English food. If the East India Company, which lorded it over the Indians, can be viewed as a precursor of the modern transnational corporation, the UK-based steel baron of Indian origins, Lakshmi Mittal, is the modern face of acquisitive British capitalism. Mittal has been on a buying spree and the Europeans do not like it one bit. With his acquisition of Arcelor, Mittal is now the largest steelmaker, and the third wealthiest person, in the world. In his own time, Robert Clive, who won India for the British in the 1750s, acquired something of a reputation as a spendthrift, but he clearly has some lessons to learn in ostentatiousness judging from the $60 million wedding Mittal arranged for his daughter in 2005.

Elsewhere in the Indian diaspora, Trinidad and Fiji have both seen the emergence, amidst the highly racialized politics of these countries, of prime ministers of Indian descent. In the same decade of the 1990s, an Indian rose to become Premier of British Columbia, and in Malaysia the Indian community was heard complaining that Ananda Krishnan had built the tallest buildings in the world, the Petronas Towers, but was uninterested in promoting the social welfare of his own people. Meanwhile, software engineers were bringing Indians into the top echelons of the American corporate world, and graduates of the Indian Institutes of Technology were being courted the world over. Once upon a time Indians were devouring the novels of Walter Scott and Charles Dickens; now, both the novel, and the English language, have been enlivened at the hands of South Asian writers of the diaspora—Vikram Seth, Amitav Ghosh, Salman Rushdie, V.S. and Shiva Naipaul, M.G. Vassanji, Harold Sonny Ladoo, Rohinton Mistry, Anita Desai, Kiran Desai, K.S. Maniam, and many others. Even Bollywood, which always had a global presence in the southern hemisphere, now seems poised to encroach upon territory that Hollywood has long since taken for granted. The diaspora is never far from Bollywood's horizon, as films such as *Dilwale Dulhaniya Le Jayenge*, *Pardes*, *Jeans*, *Kal Ho Na Ho*, *Hum Tum*, and *Kabhi Alvida Na Khaina* amply demonstrate; at the same time, in metropolises around the world, the multiplex cinema complex has provided something of a home to the Hindi film. Java, with a population exceeding 100 million, has much fewer than 100,000 Indians, but one of the central thoroughfares of Jakarta is crowned by a gigantic sculpture, inspired by the Mahabharata, of Krishna acting as the charioteer to Arjuna. These are but fragments of a story that is now beginning to be told of a comparatively small diaspora that nevertheless has inserted itself into the world's imagination.

Considering the extent to which the United States hogs the headlines, it is no surprise that its diasporic Indian population has similarly sought to position itself as the global face, not merely of overseas Indians, but even of India. The United States is today home to one of the largest Indian populations in the world, as well as to substantial diasporic Indian communities from places as far afield as Fiji, Trinidad, and Guyana. Though the presence of Indians in the U.S. can, in the main, be traced to as far back as about 1900, the contemporary history of most Indian American communities extends back to no further than four decades and the removal of restrictions that had impeded the flow of immigrants from India before the passage of new legislation in 1965. From a community then numbering in the few thousands, the Indian population has, extrapolating from the figure of 1.71 million in the 2000 census, grown to over two million. Few ethnic groups have registered such phenomenal growth, and over the last decade India has accounted for a substantial and considerable disproportionate share of both immigrant and non-immigrant visas. However, for a community that commands the highest per capita income of any racial or ethnic group, as well as the highest rate of college graduates, Indian Americans have not so far played a significant role in American politics, though signs of Indian involvement in community affairs, as well as local and state politics, are growing.

Where before Indians had made known their presence most visibly in the professions, particularly in medicine and engineering, extending in recent years to computer-related industries and investment banking, today the community is far more diversified with large numbers of Indians entering into the taxi business, fast food and convenience store franchises, and hospitality industries. The older stereotypes of Indians as doctors and engineers, of which one is often reminded when the neighbor or car mechanic adverts to the Indian origin of their physician or cardiologist, have now been joined by newer stereotypes, exemplified in Hillary Clinton's tasteless attempt at a joke in January 2004 at a fundraiser where she described Mahatma Gandhi as having run a "gas station down in St. Louis." As her equally illustrious or should we say clueless colleague in the Senate and potential Democratic Presidential candidate, Joe Biden, put it at a campaign stop in New Hampshire in July 2006, "You cannot go to a 7-Eleven or a Dunkin' Donuts unless you have a slight Indian accent. I'm not joking."

The growth and visibility of the Indian American population can, however, be marked through other developments, most obviously the rapid proliferation of Indian restaurants, the emergence of a complex and sensitive Indian (and more broadly South Asian) literature, the demarcation of Little Indias in some major metropolitan areas, the frequent invocations of Bollywood in the mass media, and even such a phenomenon, which has not been overlooked by the national media, as the unusual success of Indian American children in the National Spelling Bee. Within the Indian community, and on occasion among the more educated in the wider public, there is also awareness of the emergence of an Indian print media, the rapid increase in houses of worship (especially Hindu temples), the annual culture shows staged by Indian Student Unions across a wide spectrum of colleges and universities, the growing number of Indian students in schools and colleges, and the frequent tours of American cities by Bollywood movie stars and entertainers. These phenomena, and many others touching on the political, social, cultural, and religious lives of Indian Americans, have not generally been woven together into a cohesive history of the Indian diaspora in the United States, a history that is simultaneously attentive to the presence of subnational groups subsumed under the category of

"Indian," the numerous and often conflicting idioms in which narratives of Indian American "identity" have been written, and the geopolitics of Indianness. One might say that with the late 2006 release by Mattel Corporation of its newest Barbie, the "Diwali Festival Doll," the time has certainly come to attempt a critical history, albeit a modest one, of Indian Americans in the fullness of their political, cultural, social, religious, and economic lives.

Passage to India:
The Circulation of the Orient in America

The myriad signs of an emerging familiarity on the part of the wider American population with such diverse aspects of Indian culture, or certainly what passes for it in the diasporic setting, as Bharatnatyam, yoga, ayurveda, Hindustani instrumental music, and tandoori cooking have their antecedents in other signs of the "Orient" that were beginning to circulate in early nineteenth-century America. Among the many clichés about the intellectual exchange of ideas between the U.S. and India is that Martin Luther King derived his idea of nonviolent resistance from Mahatma Gandhi, who in turn is said to have been inspired by Henry David Thoreau's classic essay on civil disobedience. And Thoreau, if one were interested in the scholarly practice of the history of ideas, was reasonably well-steeped in classic Indian texts. Thoreau imagined that the waters of the Ganges had mingled with the equally pristine waters of Walden Pond, such that when he took a bath in its icy waters he was being washed by the stupendous cosmogonal philosophy of the Bhagavad Gita. Thoreau dedicated virtually the entirety of the "Tuesday" chapter of his *A Week on the Concord and Merrimack Rivers* to a discussion of Indian philosophical and religious treatises from which he quoted liberally.

Well before Indians first began to arrive in some numbers in the United States a little before 1900, trade had brought the products of "East India"—tea, spices, silk, muslin, opium—to New England homes. Salem owed its greatness to the commerce with the East—and now Starbucks, which rightfully augurs the importance of the West Coast as part of the Pacific Rim trading system, is unwittingly reviving long-forgotten histories with its trendy masala chai. It is the "magnificent Oriental plunder" accumulated by Elihu Yale in India, who served as a lowly clerk in the East India Company's offices before he rose to assume charge of the Madras Presidency, that lifted a New England college founded in 1676 from the doldrums and prompted its founders to rename the college in honor of the wealthy donor. As a young boy, Ralph Waldo Emerson, later to be known as the "Sage of Concord" and the leader of a group of writers and thinkers who would be characterized as the "Transcendentalists," often visited Boston's "India Wharf" which had by his time become the leading center of trade with China and India. Emerson confided to his journal in 1836 that everything in "this era" had been made "subservient" to "Trade," and "On us the most picturesque contrasts are crowded. We have the beautiful costume of the Hindoo and the Turk in our streets." Only three years previously, 100 tons of ice had successfully been shipped from Boston to Calcutta. Remarkably, ice was one of the largest revenue earners for American merchants involved in trade with India, and the Englishmen in Calcutta, Bombay, and Madras who downed their whiskies with ice were imbibing the pure waters of New England lakes and ponds.

The commerce with India aside, British colonialism had succeeded in giving India some visibility in the United States. A Christian nation was eminently interested in the spread of the gospel, and the activities of European missionaries in India were assiduously followed in the American and British press, particularly after the East India Company in 1813 began to lift restrictions on missionary activity in India. Emerson's own father, the Reverend William Emerson, authored a number of pieces on India in *The Monthly Anthology* and the *North American Review*, mainly because like other clergymen he harbored the hope that research into Oriental subjects would aid scholars investigating the origins of the Hebrew scriptures. In 1821, the younger Emerson composed a poem of 156 lines called "Indian Superstition," which is distinguished neither by its insights nor by the poet's command over verse. What notions of Hindu philosophy and religion the younger Emerson had imbibed from the work of European scholars and commentary in periodicals can be gauged from an entry in his journal, when he was but twenty years old: "The Indian Pantheon is of prodigious size; 330 million Gods have in it each their heaven, or rather, each their parlour, in this immense 'goddery.' In [its] quality and absurdity their superstition has nothing to match it, that is or ever was in the world." That was Emerson in 1823, but here is Pat Robertson on March 23, 1995, denouncing Hinduism as "demonic" on his Christian TV show, "700 Club": "Of all of India's problems, one stands out from the rest. That problem is idol worship. It is said there are hundreds of millions of Hindu deities. All this has put a nation in bondage to spiritual forces that have deceived many for thousands of years." Orientalism's most profound image, that of an "Unchanging India," to which Emerson once wholly subscribed, would appear to describe much more accurately the relentlessly inflexible outlook of some in the Western world.

The young Emerson may be excused for knowing no better, but Robertson's remarks, quite carefully calibrated rather than being a mere outburst, illustrate what American Hindus view as the veil of ignorance surrounding their faith. By the late 1830s, Emerson had graduated towards the warm embrace of some version of the perennial philosophy, and soon he would demonstrate an extraordinary partiality for Indian texts which he retained the rest of his life. "In the sleep of the great heats," he wrote to Samuel Gray Ward on July 18, 1840, "there was nothing for me to do but to read the Vedas, the bible of the tropics, which I find I come back upon every three or four years. It is sublime as heat and night and a breathless ocean. It contains every religious sentiment, all the grand ethics which visit in turn each noble and poetic mind. . ." The Vedas had made of Emerson a "Brahmin," and he drew the younger Thoreau, a fellow resident of Concord and Harvard graduate, into his circle of those who began to associate the East with enlightenment. Around the same time that a group of Boston Brahmins founded the American Oriental Society for the promotion of "Asiatic" learning and languages, Emerson initiated a journal of Transcendentalist opinion, *The Dial*, and its pages introduced readers to excerpts from "Ethnical Scriptures."

This is the groundwork into which Walt Whitman stepped when he carved his own "Passage to India" (1870). Emerson had already pre-figured the idea, which has continued to resonate in America down to the present day, if the dozens of Indian gurus at whose feet spiritually inclined Americans readily fall are a reliable indicator, that India is to the soul what the Yankee spirit is to modern science and material wealth. Whitman expanded on this notion, bemoaning the loss of soul even as he gave greater credence to rugged Yankee individualism. Meanwhile, many others were forging their own understanding and experience of India, a sentiment best expressed in the inscription that graces the statue (1868) of the Jacksonian and Democrat Senator Thomas Hart Benton (1782–1858) in St. Louis's Lafayette Square: "There is the East; there lies the road to India." One way to India had lain through the corridors of trade; another route was through the spirit. But in the last quarter of the nineteenth century, and leading into the twentieth century, another set of signs through which India could be represented received wide circulation. India was doubtless the land of magic and wonders, elephants and tigers, teeming masses and Oriental despots. Throughout, the notion of India as something of a majestic place, a land of myth, fable, grandeur and mystery, never quite disappeared from the American imagination. To the explorer Charles E. Dutton, Captain of Ordnance in the U.S. Army and author of two works on the physical geography and geology of the Grand Canyon that appeared in 1882, the incomparably "sublime" and "earthly spectacle" of the Canyon could only be rendered by naming some of its buttes and peaks after Vishnu, Shiva, Brahma, Rama, and the Hindu lawgiver, Manu. The principal butte in the "Hindoo Amphitheater," at more than 5,000 feet, was "so admirably designed and so exquisitely designed that the sight of it must call forth an expression of wonder and delight from the most apathetic beholder." Dutton, reminded of an Oriental pagoda, dubbed it "Vishnu's Temple." Its companion butte was the "grandest of all," and "the most majestic in aspect": the summit looked down 6,000 feet "into the darks depths of the inner abyss," and Dutton was reminded of the Hindu god Shiva. So came into being "the Shiva Temple." Hindu temples, one might be forgiven for thinking, have a much longer history in the U.S. than is commonly imagined.

Voyage from India:
Slaves and Seamen, Workers and Peasants

If a few Americans had since the advent of Transcendental-ism effected an imagined passage to India, Indians themselves would soon begin to make their way to the United States. Lit-tle is known about the representations of the U.S. that might have prevailed among the general public in India, or with what idea of "America" the first visitors and immigrants held forth as they took the plunge and entered into a long journey by sea. There is little to suggest that Indians had any endur-ing contacts with American visitors or that they had imbibed some definitive ideas about the United States from novels, popular literature, or travelogues. American travelers to India in the nineteenth century were predominantly missionaries or scholars, among them William Ward, author of a voluminous account of Hindu mythology and religion; the theosophist, Colonel Olcott; and the Harvard Sanskritist, Charles Lanman. But they do not appear to have been a conduit of any infor-mation about the United States to Indians. The most notable American visitor to India before the early twentieth century was perhaps Mark Twain, whose travelogue of his worldwide travels, *Following the Equator* (1896), has a memorable if nonetheless now predictable account of a country about which he thought that in it "nothing seems to have been forgotten, nothing overlooked." India was a land of "tremendous specialties," and many were the tags that had been placed upon it: "Land of the Thug, the Land of the Plague, the Land of Famine, the Land of Giant Illusions, the Land of Stupendous Mountains, and so forth." And just when one thought that one were done, India made one think of another tag, and yet another one—such that the only designation by which India could be done justice was the "all-comprehensive name," "the Land of Wonders." But there is no body of research that might suggest whether Twain's American writings, or indeed any other American literature, had found any Indian readers.

The history of Asian Indians in the United States is conventionally thought to have begun just before 1900. This history can now perhaps be pushed back to the seventeenth century. The merchant seamen employed by the East India Company who made their way to the Eastern seaboard colonies appear to have brought slaves from India, who were almost certainly unaware that they were being taken to the Americas. These slaves married into the black population, most probably converted to Christianity, and were endowed with a new name. Their story is not unlike the history of Indian slaves in Cape Town, where, though they constituted a more substantive minority of a quarter of the population, they were absorbed into more dominant categories, among them "Malay." The "East Indian" slaves in the U.S. were similarly assimilated into categories such as "mulatto," dark," and "colored," and their Christian names reveal little about their origins. One extraordinary source for this early history is the advertisements for runaway slaves and servants placed in newspapers, normally by slave owners and on occasion by county officials. The *Virginia Gazette of Williamsburg* for April 1737 mentions, for the first time, an "East-Indian," but an advertisement from August 4, 1768 in the same newspaper is not only unambiguously clear about the identity of the runaway slave but also illustrative of the difficulties of unearthing the early history of Asian Indians in the U.S.: "Richmond county, July 14. RUN away about the

20th of May last, an East-India Indian, named Thomas Green-wich." Who would be looking for an Indian by the quintessential English name of Thomas Greenwich, and just how many Indians might have been brought over as slaves? No one really knows, though if a reasonable assessment is ever made of the number of runaway Indian slaves, one might be able to extrapolate from that figure the larger sum of Indian slaves.

If research into the eighteenth-century background of Asian Indian history is in a rudimentary stage, the same must be said for most of the nineteenth century. The *Historical Statistics of the United States*, collected by the U.S. Census Bureau, may be misleading as a source for the study of early Indian immigration to the U.S. For each of the years 1820, 1822, 1824, 1826, 1827, and 1829, for example, the presence of one immigrant from India is recorded—but the phrase "from India" deserves careful scrutiny, since in each of these years the immigrant only reported India as the last place of his permanent residence. These immigrants may have been Anglo-Indians, or even Britishers availing themselves of their freedom of movement within an Anglophonic sphere of influence. A study of the original muster rolls from the Civil War period at the National Archives suggests that Indians and Malays joined the Chinese in serving in the Union Army and especially Union Navy during the Civil War, but research on this question is at a very preliminary stage. Customjee Rustomjee, who hailed from an aristocratic family from Lahore, made his way to the U.S. around the 1850s, converted to Christianity when he came under the tutelage of the Reverend Ward Beecher, and served on at least two different warships in the Union Navy during the Civil War. It is as Antonio Gomez that he is now known to history: he worked for the U.S. Navy the rest of his adult life, settled down in San Francisco, and apparently was buried with full military honors upon his death in 1911. In the latter part of the nineteenth century, a handful of Indians had meanwhile made an appearance in the United States. Among the earliest visitors to the U.S. from India were Anindibai Joshi, the first Indian woman to earn an MD from an American medical school, and the equally remarkable Pandita Ramabai, an indefatigable social reformer whose *The High Caste Hindu Woman* (1888) would later be decried as a work which had contributed disproportionately to the idea that Indian women suffered under the crushing weight of an oppressive patriarchy.

The first significant presence of Indians in the United States can be dated to 1899-1900 and the subsequent decade. Four Indian soldiers who had served in the British Royal Artillery in Hong Kong were given permission to land and settle in San Francisco in early April 1899. The *San Francisco Chronicle* described them as having left their ancestral home in Lahore [now in Pakistan] some twenty years ago, and opined that they "are all fine-looking men, Bakkshlled [sic] Singh in particular being a marvel of physical beauty." A trickle of peasants from the province of Punjab were to make their way to the West Coast, seeking work in Washington's lumber mills and California's vast agricultural fields. If no Statue of Liberty stood near the shore to greet Indians, no laws prevented their immigration into America or precluded them from striving to enhance their economic prospects in life. The Naturalization Act of 1790 allowed only "free white persons" to become U.S. citizens, and legislation in 1870 extended this privilege to people of African descent. A series of measures enacted by the California Legislature—among them, the California Foreign Miners Tax of 1850; the exclusion of Chinese from San Francisco's public schools, effective 1859; exclusion from 1870 onwards of the wives of Chinese laborers; the Page Law of 1875, which barred the entry into the U.S. of Japanese, Chinese, and "Mongolian" felons, prostitutes, and contract laborers; and the Chinese Exclusion Act of 1882, upheld in *Chae Chan Ping* v. *U.S.* (1889), which suspended immigration of Chinese laborers for ten years and excluded the Chinese from obtaining citizenship by naturalization—had already placed restrictions on other Asians, but it is not known whether Indians were even aware of such developments. Moreover, this first significant wave of Indian immigration would coincide with America's expansion as an imperial power. The Spanish-American War turned the Philippines into an American protectorate and in 1898 Hawaii was annexed by the United States.

Ironically, just as Indians were about to make their presence known in the United States, efforts were being made to restrict their ability to put down roots in South Africa. Mohandas Gandhi, later to become renowned as the Mahatma, had arrived there in 1893 at the invitation of an Indian merchant to assist him in a law case, and he at once encountered racial discrimination. When four years later the young Mohandas sought to bring his wife and children to South Africa, a white mob gathered at the docks in Durban and attempted to prevent him and several hundred other free Indians from landing. Loud voices were raised within the European community seeking an end to Indian immigration into South Africa, but others, including the Secretary of State for the Colonies, Joseph Chamberlain, argued that the exclusion of Indians, who were also subjects of Queen Victoria, on grounds of their race was too blatantly discriminatory and would seriously jeopardize British claims that the Empire was in some respects a hospitable home for all. It was idle to pretend, of course, that Indians were equal to whites: but if their exclusion was sought, it had to be done on some other pretext. The British colony of Natal devised an appropriate strategy, requiring Asian immigrants to demonstrate literacy in a European language, and Colonial Secretary Joseph Chamberlain advocated the "Natal formula" at a meeting of colonial prime ministers in London in 1897 as the most desirable solution to protect settler colonies from "the invasion of the class to which they would justly object." Indeed, exclusionists in the United States, Australasia, Canada, and South Africa shared, through formal and informal networks, information with each other about the various methods used in their domains to restrict immigration of Asians.

With the concatenation of these circumstances serving as the backdrop, Asian Indians slowly started trickling into the United States. Though for the first few years the migrants were predominantly Sikhs, they were described as "Hindus" or more commonly "Hindoos," and indeed the U.S. Immigration Commission of 1911 held that any native of India was, for immigration purposes, to be viewed as a "Hindu." They came largely from the Jullunder and Hoshiarpur districts of the Punjab, a land which by the mid-nineteenth century had acquired in British Indian writings something of an iconographic status. British officials held to the view that the Punjab was a distinct repository of India's rural traditions, and that the Punjabi was both childlike and an authentic specimen of a manhood rarely encountered in India. The reorganization of the Indian Army after the ferocious fighting which ensued during the Indian Rebellion of 1857–1858 led to an enhanced role for Punjabis, especially Sikhs, in the army as they were construed as a people who subscribed to genuine martial traditions and were cognizant of the values of loyalty and obedience. By the late nineteenth century, Sikh soldiers had served in various outposts of the British empire, and were to be found throughout Southeast Asia and Shanghai. Some, disillusioned with, or simply retired from, army service created a niche for themselves as doormen and policemen, occupations with which they are still associated in Singapore and Hong Kong. In the Punjab itself, grim economic conditions furnished additional incentive to leave for more promising economic opportunities. For the Punjabis, as for millions of people around the world, America beckoned: a world wide web of rumors had firmly established a place for the "land of milk and honey" in the global imaginary.

Some 2,050 persons from India are reported in the census as residing in the U.S. in 1900. The phrase "from India" is significant, as this number, which includes Anglo-Indians, bears little relation to the number of people of Indian origin known to have been admitted into the U.S. until around 1910, averaging perhaps around 150 per year. Two hundred and fifty-eight Indians were admitted in 1904, 145 in 1905, and 271 in 1906. By 1907, Bellingham in Washington state had several hundred Indians employed in lumber mills. The Western Pacific Railway in northern California, a transcontinental line built across the Sierra, provided another substantial source of employment. However, an increasing number of Indians were turning to agricultural labor. California's agriculture industry had been experiencing labor shortages, and as early as 1874 a writer for the *Pacific Commercial Advertiser*, perhaps familiar with the deployment of Indian labor in British colonies around the world, had suggested turning towards India: "Where shall we look for the kind of immigrants we need to supply us with both a homogeneous population and labor? We answer, to the East Indies. From the teeming millions of Bengal and other provinces of Hindostan." When Punjabi farmers finally arrived in the United States nearly three decades later, they encountered farming conditions, from the alluvial soil to irrigation techniques, with which they were already familiar. They generally worked together in gangs and practiced cooperative land leasing. As in the lumber industry, the Indians were initially viewed as a reliable pool of labor, inclined to save money, and not overly demanding; indeed, as in the lumber industry, where employers paid Indians $2.00 for a day's labor instead of the set wage of $2.22, so on the farms the employers typically underpaid the Indian peasants. The United States Immigration Commission in its report of 1909 confirmed that it was "practically universal to discriminate against the East Indian in wages."

Those seeking entry into the U.S. from Vancouver had perhaps constituted the most sizable pool of Indians who in the early 1900s were settling down on the west coast. Traveling by ship from India, the Sikhs made their way to Hong Kong, where a Gurdwara had been established in 1901, or to Penang and Singapore; and from there a ship brought them to Vancouver. In 1906, Vancouver was shaken by an anti-Asian riot, and two years later Canada barred all entry to Indians. An exception was allowed for those Indians who had made a "continuous journey" to Canada from India, but since such a journey could not in fact be undertaken, the exception pointed to an illusory degree of magnanimity. Canada was now out of bounds for Indians, and they gravitated towards the United States, to which they had unimpeded access if they could pass a physical examination administered at the border, and where, as has been suggested, farm land—in the San Joaquin, Sacramento, and Imperial valleys in California—was, or so it seemed, readily available. Indians would not have recognized that, though they had been in the U.S. for less than a decade, the doors were slowly starting to close in on them; or, swayed like everyone else by the mythography of an endlessly open American frontier, they did not wish to read the signs appearing before them.

Though Indians led generally unobtrusive lives, oral histories and anecdotal evidence unequivocally suggest creeping discrimination, and most certainly the assimilation of Indians into a mix of overwhelming stereotypes. One early Sikh immigrant many years later recounted how a white man emerging from a bar motioned to him, "'Come here, slave!' I said I was no slave man. He told me that his race ruled India and America, too. All we were slaves. He came close to me and I hit him and got away fast." At a camp set up next to an agricultural field, where laborers dined and slept through the night, an exchange that reportedly once took place between a Sikh and a woman described as a "visiting lady" is illustrative both of the preconceptions surrounding Indians and the humor and alertness with which they sought to navigate their way in white society. The Indian laborer explained to her, "We eat no meat, that is no beef—the cow is sacred." To this the woman is said to have issued this sharp rejoinder: "But you drink milk? And your cow gives you the milk!" She could not have expected this riposte: "Yes, we drink our mother's milk also, but we do not eat her!" Not all exchanges were this harmless, and some of the dominant stereotypes would become critical in the minds of policymakers. In 1920, as the "Oriental Question" had come to assume a pivotal importance in public discourse, the Chief Sanitary Engineer for the State Commission of Immigration and Housing reported that the "Hindu standard of living is so vastly different from ours that it is difficult to present it properly. Their methods of preparing food and serving is [sic] very primitive. Dishes, pots and pans are unnecessary in the life of a Hindu. Sanitary conveniences are unknown."

That trickle of several hundred Indians must at any rate have appeared to white America as a deluge since calls for their removal would begin surfacing in the press and among American labor leaders long before the first decade of the twentieth century was over. From nearly the outset they were seen as unassimilable, possessed of "immodest and filthy habits," and regarded as the "most undesirable, of all the eastern Asiatic races." The title of an article by Fred Lockley appearing in the May 1907 issue of the *Pacific Monthly* tells the story in the most succinct terms: "The Hindu Invasion: A New Immigration Problem." Several hundred thousand Britishers, with whom many Americans shared their ancestry, had forcibly imposed themselves upon Indians but their acts of self-aggrandizement elicited no comments from white Americans, much less any criticism; and yet a miniscule number of Indians, most of them Sikhs but all rendered into a generic category called "Hindus," had now been transformed into the vanguard of invading hordes. If the word "new" in Lockley's article signaled to the reader that Hindus constituted the latest iteration of troublesome Asians making their way to the United States, the appearance of the word "problem" rested on the old canard, which is present in every debate on immigration that has taken place in American society, that Indians were not only unassimilable but were undercutting wages of agricultural labor. Lockley had evidently chosen his words wisely: soon the cormorant crew of harpies was at work, and in quick succession appeared these and other like pieces: "The West and the Hindu Invasion," *Overland Monthly* (1908); "Hindu Invasion," *Collier's Magazine* (1910); and "The Hindu, the Newest Immigration Problem," *Survey* (1910). Once an invasion has occurred, it must, sooner or later, be repelled.

In two separate incidents in 1907, both in the state of Washington, Indians were subjected to racial attacks and compelled to seek protective custody. Towards the end of August, mill workers in Bellingham were warned by union leaders that they were not to employ Indians, often described in the popular press as "rag-heads." Though even most Sikhs turned to Western dress, they were still distinguished by their flowing beards and turbans and more likely to attract attention than other Asians. In the main incident on September 4th, a crowd of around 500 men surrounded the mills and boarding houses where Indians were gathered and started pelting them with rocks. The local newspaper, the *Morning Reveille*, noted that the "small police force was overpowered" and in the fracas many

Indians were hurt. They were given notice that they must leave Bellingham; the next day, about 300 Indian laborers quit town. Meeting in San Francisco in February 1908, the Asiatic Exclusion League declared that from everywhere in coastal California complaints "are made of the undesirability of the Hindoos, their lack of cleanliness, disregard of sanitary laws, petty pilfering, especially of chickens, and insolence to women."

The juggernaut of anti-Hindu sentiment had been set rolling: Samuel Gompers, the president of the American Federation of Labor, on whose behalf one can say at least that he was multicultural in his equal disdain for all Asiatics, gave it as his considered opinion that "sixty years" contact with the Chinese, twenty-five years' experience with the Japanese and two or three years' acquaintance with Hindus should be sufficient to convince any ordinarily intelligent person that they have no standards. . . by which a Caucasian may judge them." These remarks appeared in his polemic, "Meat vs. Rice: American Manhood Against Asiatic Coolieism." Every word in this title is pregnant with meaning: if American, manhood, and meat operate as appositional terms as do Asiatic, coolieism, and rice in this narrative, each set obviously also stands in oppositional relationship to the other set. In the seventeenth century, Montesquieu had already furnished the contours for a climatic determinism by distinguishing between cultures on the basis of their staple grain. When in the late eighteenth century Robert Orme penned what was to become the classic exposition of its kind, "On the Effeminacy of the Inhabitants of Hindustan," he argued that rice-growing and rice-consuming people such as the Hindus did not have to expend much labor and were consequently inclined to laziness and moral turpitude. The young Mohandas Gandhi was but a schoolboy when he heard the doggerel, then very much in vogue in his native Gujarat:

> Behold the mighty Englishman
> He rules the Indian small,
> Because being a meat-eater
> He is five cubits tall.

One might say that Gompers was hearkening back to all

these accumulated traditions. He would have remained clueless about how the staunchly vegetarian Gandhi, whose experiments in meat-eating were short-lived, became the principal architect of the Indian independence movement, or how the rice-eating Vietnamese defeated, later in the century, the mightiest military force known to humankind.

Within a few years after the arrival of Indians in the United States, concerted attempts would be made by the Asiatic Exclusion League—formerly the Japanese and Korean Exclusion League, and renamed in 1905 to reflect the new "menace"—and other associations to prevent further immigration from India into the United States, to intimidate those already in the country into abandoning the U.S., and to restrict their capacity to own property. Once Bellingham had set the example, other towns felt similarly emboldened. The white lumbermen of the inaptly named town of Saint John, just outside Portland, Oregon, succeeded in driving out its Hindu workers. Indians suffered the same fate in Everest. But perhaps the greater alarm bells were sounded by the *San Francisco Chronicle*, which in its issue of September 29, 1910 warned that reports of Hindu men sending for their wives in India could not be ignored. If the readers of the *Chronicle* knew anything at all about "Hindus," it was that they bred rapidly, and what could be the purpose of wives joining husbands if not to give rise to progeny? In these circumstances, the new immigrants, whose difficulties were compounded by their relatively high illiteracy rates, their poor knowledge of English, and their lack of wider sociopolitical networks, undoubtedly imbibed their first political lessons, acquiring the skills and tenacity necessary to combat racism, pursue a livelihood, and—as shall be seen—work the courts to gain reprieve.

The Diaspora within the Diaspora:
Students and Rebels

Two other classes of Indians had begun to make their way to the United States alongside the former soldiers who had served the British Empire and the more numerous Punjabi farmers and laborers. The first Indian student arrived in 1901, and in less than a decade a small body of Indian male students had congregated at UC Berkeley, the polytechnic at San Luis Obispo, CA and a few agricultural colleges. Berkeley is said to have had the largest body of Indian students, and strikingly in 1911 one of its students, Sarangadhar Das, published a lengthy article in the well-known Calcutta-based journal of intellectual opinion, *The Modern Review*, which served as something of a handbook for students in India contemplating a course of study at Berkeley and eager to be apprised about living conditions in California. Das's guide disguises as much as it reveals, shrewdly remaining silent on the political activities in which some Indian students had begun to be engaged.

It is not America which radicalized these students, though for some years it furnished a fertile ground for their activities. Anti-British revolutionary activity had been picking up steam in India since the late 1890s, and events of the subsequent decade forced Indian radicals to consider overseas sites from which they could continue to agitate for Indian independence. The partition of Bengal in 1905 by the British administration had the effect of giving rise to concerted opposition, animated by aspirations for self-reliance and autonomy, encompassed under the Indian term "swadeshi" [of one's own country]. Not surprisingly, British repression increased and the Criminal Law Amendment of 1908 put into force more draconian measures for the containment of what the British described as terrorism and revolutionary extremism. Meanwhile, Japan's decisive military triumph over Russia in 1905 had electrified Indian nationalists: not only did it shatter the pretensions of European supremacy, but it gave rise to the thought that the world was about to witness a new phase in the resurgence of Asian civilizations. There is increasing evidence of the emergence of Tokyo in the beginning of the twentieth century as the site of radical movements in pan-Asianism and revolutionary socialism. However, if Japan beckoned and the lure of a common Asiatic bond could not be resisted, Indian students soon discovered that the Japanese had absolutely no commitment to the idea of the equality of races. By 1907, reports began to appear in the Indian press of Indian students in Japan who complained of rude treatment at the hands of their hosts, and the influential newspaper, *The Bengalee*, stated candidly in its issue of August 2, 1907: "Before the Russo-Japanese war there was hardly any topic on which the Japanese press and statesmen waxed more eloquent than the pan-Asiatic movement and the upheaval of all the nations of Asia. Her Korean policy, therefore, has come as a great surprise upon the Asiatic public."

Surendra Mohan Bose was one among those disaffected Indian students who made his way from Tokyo, where he had helped establish "India House," to Vancouver in 1907 and from there to the United States, where in 1913 he became General Secretary of the Hindustan Association of the United States. A senior British official who compiled records of "Criminal Intelligence" for India's colonial government wrote of Bose that he passed on instructions on how to make bombs to an associate in Vancouver before leaving for Paris, where Indian revolutionaries had been active since at least early 1909. In 1907, the strident anticolonialist Madame Rustomji Cama, who since 1902 had been living in Scotland, London, Germany, and Paris, took some students with her to the Socialist International Conference at Stuttgart, where she unfurled the Indian flag and denounced British rule in India; that same year, she visited the United States and again advocated Indian independence. "We are in slavery," she informed her New York audience, "and I am in America for the sole purpose of giving a thorough exposé of the British oppression, which is little understood so far away, and to interest the warmhearted citizens of this great Republic in our enfranchisement." Eventually, in 1909, Madame Cama made her home in Paris, where a circle of revolutionaries gathered around her and the nationalist S.R. Rana, with whom she co-edited a nationalist newspaper, *Bande Mataram*.

If this were not enough, Indian students and nationalists in the U.S. found that they could make common cause with Irish anti-imperialists active on the East Coast. The visit to the U.S. of the renowned nationalist leader, Lala Lajpat Rai, in 1905 underscored the importance that he and other informed leaders ascribed to forging wider alliances in opposition to British colonialism. Lajpat Rai addressed the Boston Anti-Imperialist League in an endeavor to awaken Americans to the realities of British oppression in India and gain worldwide recognition for India's quest for home rule. The December 1905 issue of the *Gaelic American* featured an article entitled "India and Ireland Working Together." Months later, Samuel Lucas Joshi, a Maharashtrian Christian, and Mahomed Barakatullah, who came from the central Indian city of Muslim culture, Bhopal, together founded the Pan-Aryan Association. On its heels came the Indo-American National Association, which would soon be renamed "Society for the Advancement of India." Neither organization survived very long, though they mark the originary moment of Indian institutions in the United States, and the New York-based revolutionaries dispersed: Joshi and some others went to India, and Barakatullah left for Japan.

Shyamaji Krishnavarma, an Oxford-educated Gujarati

known to the British as the head of the conspiracy to rob them of their Indian possessions, had long been fomenting a plan that would enable "authors, journalists, and other qualified Indians to visit Europe, America and other parts of the world beyond the limits of India, so as to equip themselves efficiently for the work of spreading among the people of India a knowledge of freedom and national unity." Little did he know how his dream would come to fruition. London, Paris, New York, Berkeley, San Francisco, Vancouver, Tokyo: these were the nodal points around which nationalists, seditionists, and radical and disaffected students circulated, sowing the ground for a far-reaching revolutionary movement aimed at dislodging the British from India. Even the students who steered clear of political activity would have been aware both of political developments in India and of the presence of political radicals and dissenters in their midst on the West Coast. By the second decade of the twentieth century, a sufficiently large coterie of cosmopolitan Indian rebels, whose ranks would be swelled and complicated by peasants and workers who had experienced the piercing effects of racial discrimination, felt emboldened enough to initiate a political party to press for Indian independence from British rule. The "Hindi Association of the Pacific Coast" took root in 1913, founded in Oregon; but it is by the name of Ghadr (also Ghadar, "revolutionary" or "mutiny") that it is commonly known. The "Ghadar Conspiracy," as the British termed it, lasted a mere five years; the journal by the same name, which was immediately conceived as the vehicle for the expression of the group's ideas, effectively ceased publication after four years, though an occasional irregular issue would continue to be published until 1929. Yet the Ghadr movement would become a diaspora within a diaspora: even as the Indian diaspora had already assumed global dimensions, the watchword of Ghadr spread like wildfire and branches of the party became established, or found supporters, in Afghanistan, China, Japan, Java, Malaya, Sumatra, Thailand (Siam), Singapore, the Philippines, Argentina, Brazil, Panama, East Africa, South Africa, France, and elsewhere.

The Ghadr party's leadership points to the multiple origins of the movement and the diverse strands that fed into its ideology. Its President was Baba Sohan Singh Bakhna, who had arrived in the U.S. as a laborer in 1909, but the editor of the party newspaper, Lala Har Dayal, was a student at Berkeley who commenced his advanced studies in 1912. Some of the party's ideologues, such as Ram Chandra, wrote at great length; others, such as Taraknath Das, who enrolled as a student at University of Washington in Seattle in 1906 and then moved on to Berkeley in 1912 for his PhD, would continue to play an influential role in the affairs of the Indian American community over the next few decades. (Taraknath eventually earned his PhD from Georgetown in 1924, and he was among the first Indians to serve as an educator in the United States.) But it is the Ghadr's party newspaper which most of all suggests why the romance with the Ghadr movement among Indian progressives endures. The masthead—across which were blazoned the words, "the enemy of the British Raj"—of the inaugural issue of *Ghadr*, published from Yugantar ["New Era"] Ashram, San Francisco on November 1, 1913, gave more than adequate clues about the intent of its founders:

> What is our name?
> Ghadr.
> In what does our work consist?
> In bringing about a rising.
> Where will this Ghadr break out?
> In India.
> When will it break out?
> In a few years.
> Why will it take place?
> Because the people can no longer bear the oppression and tyranny practiced under English rule and are ready to fight and die for freedom. It is the duty of every Indian to make preparations for this rising.

Published at first in Urdu, the predominant language (alongside Hindustani) of north India, and Gurmukhi, the language of Punjabi peasants, *Ghadr* within months had also commenced publication in Gujarati and Hindi. A contemporary British intelligence report confirmed that some 3,000 copies of the paper were mailed to the Federated Malay States, Siam, and elsewhere in Asia and that it was reasonable to infer that "the whole circulation of the paper at this time must have reached a formidable degree." When one contemplates that nearly 100 years ago an Indian newspaper was being published from the United States in at least four languages, though there are reports of its irregular publication in several more languages, including English, Bengali, and Pashto, one marvels at the ecumenism, grit, ambition, and vision of the movement's advocates—and all this without any pretensions at "multiculturalism." From time to time supplements appeared to Ghadr: one such pamphlet, entitled *Jang da Hoka* ("Declaration of War"), declaimed against the "feringhees" (foreigners) who had taken possession of India, engaged in rapine and destruction, spread "famine, plague and malaria" in the country, and forced Indians to emigrate to fill their stomachs—and then, to rub salt into their wounds, attempted to influence the Governments of Australia, Canada, [South] Africa and America to prevent the entry of Indians into these countries. In the "Wanted" section of the newspaper, the Ghadrites published this tidbit:

> Wanted: Revolutionaries.
> Job: To launch Ghadr (revolution).
> Pay: Martyrdom
> Pension: Liberty
> Field of Battle: Hindustan

The Ghadr poets, as the folklorist and longtime Berkeley resident Ved Prakash Vatuk has suggested, chafed at the humiliations imposed upon their countrymen in the U.S., and their call of protest resonated with Indians—in the U.S., India, and in British possessions around the world—who at once understood what it meant to be called a coolie, or to have to face signs at shop windows which unabashedly declared: "No entry for Indians or dogs." In the words of one Ghadr poet:

> We are faced with innumerable miseries
> We are called coolies and thieves
> Wherever we go we are treated like dogs.

Adherents of the Ghadr Party set for themselves the goal of liberating India by all means at their disposal, and from the United States some returned after the outbreak of war to India, in the colorful language of British officials, to foment trouble, consort with the Germans, and lure the peasantry into rebellion. They certainly appear to have been both somewhat misled and optimistic about the state of revolutionary activity in India, not fully realizing that conditions for full-fledged insurrectionary activity throughout India were far from being ripe. An early attempt in 1915 to influence political events in India was foiled when a large shipment of guns, ammunition, and propaganda literature destined for India was intercepted by the British. America's entry into the war in 1917 sealed the fate of the Ghadrites: acting under relentless pressure from the British, an intensive and successful prosecution was launched against them for conspiring with the Germans to illegally deprive the British monarch of his sovereignty over India. However, to make the charges stick, it was necessary to demonstrate that the Indians had violated "the laws and hospitality" of the United States, indeed given comfort and shelter to its sworn enemies, by consorting with the Germans against whom the U.S. was now at war. The "Hindu German Conspiracy Trial," as it was dubbed in the press, was not without high drama: towards the conclusion of the trial in April 1918, one of the defendants, Ram Chandra, was shot dead in court by another defendant, Ram Singh, who in turn was killed on the spot by a policeman.

There is something at once poignant and inspiring in the narrative of the Ghadr movement. Its adherents, traveling on criss-crossing paths, moving between India, European capitals, Tokyo, the Malay world, and North America, had attempted to bind together the United States and India in a curious relationship. The political radicals and rebels in the movement had fled India in the belief that they would encounter greater political freedom in the United States, where they arrived to find themselves confronted with openly racist sentiments and even racial violence. The passage of the Alienation of Land Act (1900) in Punjab, which had placed restrictions on the ownership of agricultural land among non-farming castes, now appeared to Punjabis who had made their way to the U.S. to prefigure the disabilities from which they and other Asians would suffer after the passage of the Alien Land Law in California in 1913. Thus the Ghadr movement drew unto its fold political rebels, students, intellectuals, workers, and farmers, a rare accomplishment unto itself, and one all the more remarkable in that it was ecumenical enough to attract Sikhs, Hindus, and Muslims. One might argue that it is only at a great remove from India that the Ghadrites could entertain, with the rather greater ease that is possible when complex intertwined histories of the past do not forcibly encroach upon the present, the utopian notion of a mother India that would be freed by militant action. The sociologist Mark Juergensmeyer coined the phrase "Gadar syndrome" to describe the phenomenon of a "militant nationalist movement" created "abroad by expatriates," embodying "the fusion and the mutual interaction of ethnic anger and nationalist pride." In the comparatively more recent language of Benedict Anderson, the Ghadr movement appears to exemplify all the strands of "long-distance nationalism." Useful as are these ideas, they do not entirely capture the globalizing energy of Ghadr, much less the magisterial manner in which the Ghadr movement anticipated the notion of a global Indian diaspora. The Ghadrites, I am tempted to say after Bruce Chatwin, drew their own songlines across the oceans, and everywhere provided assurance to Indians that Indianness was, in some fashion, theirs to claim.

"Tawnies" Amidst Whites
(after Benjamin Franklin)

Canada had, as we have seen, slammed shut its doors to Indians in 1908, and only in 1947, when India attained independence, were restrictions on entry of Indians lifted. The population of 5,000 Indians in 1908 had dwindled to around 700 by 1918. Though the history of Indians in Canada constitutes its own distinct chapter in the narrative of the global Indian diaspora, immigrants saw the border in the early years of the twentieth century as porous and British officials in India were similarly alarmed at the apparent ease with which Indians moved back and forth between Vancouver and the northwest United States. Borders exist to be transgressed, but this thought was as far from the mind of officials then as it is from the minds of those who today seek to halt so-called illegal immigrants from Mexico. The British official in the Central Intelligence Office of the Indian Government's Home Department who in 1914 wrote that the "students at Berkeley, California, are also [besides the Sikhs] believed to be almost universally tainted with Ghadar ideas" added this note: "Prima facie, every Indian returning from America or Canada, whether labourer, artisan or student, must be regarded with the greatest suspicion as a probable active revolutionary, or at any rate as a sympathizer with the revolutionary."

The calamitous incident of the *Komagata Maru*, though it did not involve Indians in the U.S., left a vivid impression on Indians around the world and especially across the border from Canada. The Indo-Canadian Sikh leader, Gurdit Singh, set out to test the "continuous journey" rule which Canadian immigration officials had imposed upon Indians, and he hired a Japanese-owned ship to ferry 376 Indians directly to Vancouver from Hong Kong. Having satisfied the "continuous journey" requirement, the Indians as British subjects should have been allowed entry into Canada. But Canadian officials kept the ship at bay for two months after its arrival in Vancouver, refusing its passengers permission to disembark. With the greater bulk of its passengers, one of whom had died from illness, still on board, the ship was forced to sail back to Calcutta, where police firing, arising not merely from a misunderstanding and frayed nerves but from the perception that the Indians on board were tainted with revolutionary ideas, would take the lives of twenty passengers.

In the United States, calls emanating from labor leaders and the wider public to keep out the "Hindoos" had been escalating. In principle, at least, American officials were prepared to resist such calls, particularly since the need for migrant labor on farms and railway tracks had not diminished. Congress was not receptive to legislative proposals to keep out Indians, most particularly because Indian immigration to the U.S., far from being a national concern, was still overwhelmingly confined to the West Coast. Officials of the Immigration and Naturalization Bureau, however, were much less reluctant to exercise their discretion in keeping out "undesirables." The Commissioner of Immigration at San Francisco issued strict orders in 1910 that an Indian seeking admission into the U.S. was to be denied entry if he was likely to become a public charge or if he could not pass an "exacting physical examination." His counterpart at Seattle went considerably further, as these passages from his annual report in 1910 amply testify: "A number of Hindus have applied for admission to the United States through this district during the year just passed. *Every Hindu has been rejected* by the board of special inquiry on the ground of belief in polygamy, likely to become a public charge, doctor's certificate, or as an assisted immigrant" (emphasis added). In 1906, only 8 percent of all Indians who had sought entry into the U.S. had been debarred; but three years later, a full 50 percent of Indians were unable to gain entry. In 1915, with the British weighing down on the Americans to assist them in the suppression of immigrant insurrectionary activity, only one out of every five Indians was allowed entry. Between 1911 and 1920, nearly 1460 Indians were admitted, but it is less often recognized that 1,782 Indians were prevented from entering the U.S. during the same period. Whatever the supposed ideals of the great American Republic, even at a time when Indians faced no legal hurdles in entering the United States more of them were disallowed rather than permitted entry. Not less significantly, the number of Indians who sought admission showed a drastic decline, from 2,193 in 1910 to 1,378 the following year and to a mere 386 in 1915.

Even as Indian immigration had been effectively curtailed, the Immigration Bureau sought a more lasting and legislative solution to the "Oriental problem." An American immigration official admitted in 1914 that the "safest" plan "to preclude the possibility of a Hindu invasion is for Congress to enact a suitable exclusion law." The Supreme Court's decision in *Plessy* v. *Ferguson* (1896), which affirmed the constitutionality of state-imposed racial segregation and provided legal sanction to the "One Drop" rule, clearly showed that exclusion could take many forms. The "One Drop" rule imposed a new rule of thumb: a single drop of blood or ancestry from Africa was enough to make a person *not* white. Had this rule been in place in the eighteenth century, it is doubtful that any of the founding fathers would have passed muster; at the other end, African American activists in the twentieth century and since have recognized that a principle of exclusion can be turned on its head to stake a new ethos of inclusion. This unsavory history suggests, at any rate, why the struggle for equality waged by Indian Americans, and more broadly Asian Americans, cannot be divorced from the same struggle in which African Americans have been engaged since the seventeenth century. Though people of African descent had become eligible for citizenship in 1870, they could not exercise the franchise and remained, in every respect, subjugated to the dominant white society. Some people were outright excluded, forbidden entry into the United States; the chimera of citizenship circumscribed the lives of others. A foreign power such as Japan could seek some favors for its citizens that were denied to the Chinese, but even then it found that it could not operate outside the idiom of exclusion which constitutes the definitive history of the United States at this time. Under the "Gentleman's Agreement" of 1907, Japan agreed that it would no longer permit laborers to emigrate to the United States. Two years later California passed legislation which added the Japanese to the list of people forbidden from marrying whites.

The very short-lived status of the Japanese as a superior breed of Asians would finally be altogether undermined in 1917. The aspirations of all Asians, including Indians, keen to shape their future in the United States received a massive setback that year with the passage of the Barred Zone Act of February 4, 1917, which "barred" *all immigrants* from areas east of the 50th meridian and west of the 110th meridian from entering the United States. Even as the United States would abandon its isolationist course and enter the First World War to secure the world from despotism and gallantly proclaim itself as the savior of democracy, it was saving itself *from* democracy. Benjamin Franklin's colorful ruminations on the true color of America, encountered in his 1751 essay *Observations Concerning the Increase of Mankind, Peopling of Countries, etc.*, suggest why we should not be surprised at the series of legislative and popular measures culminating in the Immigration Act of 1917. The Saxons and English, he noted, constituted the "principal Body of White People on the Face of the Earth"—though, as the text suggests, he meant "principle," people of integrity and honor, as much as "principal." Franklin objected to the peopling of America by tawny-colored immigrants: "Why increase the Sons of Africa," he asked, "by Planting them in America, where we have so fair an opportunity, by excluding all Blacks and Tawneys, of increasing the lovely White and Red?" That alleged radical, Thomas Jefferson, was in something of a quandary because of this wretched question of color. "The improvement of the blacks in body and mind," he wrote in *Notes on the State of Virginia*, "in the first instance of their mixture with the whites, has been observed by every one, and proves that their inferiority is not the effect merely of their condition of life." While he was committed to improving the lives of black people, he was also desirous of seeing America blossom with the seed of white people and was eventually led to the conclusion that the relocation of blacks to another country was best calculated to serve the interests of the new society being shaped in the United States. Oh lovely white people, what knots do you tie yourselves in?

While the legislation of 1917 was effective in barring Asians from further entry into the United States, it did not expressly prohibit Indians from applying for citizenship. Nor did it help to settle the ambiguity surrounding the idea of "white" or "whiteness." At this time the privilege of naturalized citizenship was for whites alone to claim, though the conflation of white with "Aryan" and "Caucasian" had by no means been resolved. When, around 1905–1906, Indians for the first time applied for American citizenship, no one quite knew how to adjudicate their applications. The Justice Department in 1907 first stated that it could "not venture to express an opinion" on this question, but on being pressed to enumerate the nationalities that came "within the term white person," Attorney General Charles Bonaparte replied on August 14: "It seems to me clear that under no construction of the law can natives of British India be regarded as white persons." However, Bonaparte's views were not binding on courts, and at least one judge, in Savannah, Georgia, asked the Afghan merchant Abdullah Dolla, who had filed a petition for citizenship, to roll up his sleeves. The blue veins on Dolla's arms persuaded the judge that Dolla was "white," certainly, one might say, much more white than black. A ruling on somewhat more substantive grounds was delivered the following year in a case that had come before the Federal Court of Appeals on the citizenship status of a Parsi from Bombay, Bhicaji Franji Balsara. The U.S. government, which opposed Balsara's petition in federal court, claimed that the word "white" could only be used apropos of the races which had been settled in the country before the American Revolution and had thus contributed to the establishment of the United States. While the court declared itself unpersuaded by this argument, it again left the meaning of the phrase, "free white persons," open to interpretation by its willingness to "confer the privilege of naturalization upon members of the white or Caucasian race only." At the appeal level, the Court clarified that Congress had meant to designate the "Caucasian" race by the word "white." And Parsis, claiming Persia as their ancestral land, were doubtless white. In the case of Ahkoy Kumar Mozumdar (1913), the court extended the meaning of Caucasian to "high-caste Hindu[s] of pure blood."

The Census of 1910 devised six categories to classify the population of the United States: White, Negro, American Indian, Japanese, Chinese, and Other. Notwithstanding the fact that some courts had already admitted Indians to citizenship, Hindus—which we must recall was the generic term for Indians—were placed in the category of the "Other" since, as one official document argued, "the popular conception of the term "white" is doubtless largely determined by the fact that the whites in this country are almost exclusively Caucasians of European origin." The classification remained intact, and did nothing to diminish the confusion. Throughout the second decade, some judges were sympathetic to citizenship claims filed by Indians, while others expressed incredulity at the suggestion that white could mean anything other than "white European." Between 1907 and 1922, about seventy Indians were admitted to citizenship. Things came to a head with the Supreme Court's November 1922 decision in the case of Takao Ozawa, a Japanese fluent in English and resident in the United States for twenty years whose application for citizenship was opposed by the government on the grounds that he was not white. Justice

Sutherland, in stipulating that "white" ought to be interpreted to mean "Caucasian," appeared to confirm earlier rulings. Sutherland's decision explicitly took note of the application of the word "Caucasian" to Indians, and was received with much jubilation by Indians who, viewing themselves as Caucasians, indeed as representatives of the oldest branch of the Aryan family, clearly were not thinking of pan-Asian identities.

Whatever satisfaction Indians may have received from the Ozawa decision, the celebration would be short-lived. In early 1923, the Supreme Court heard on appeal from the Immigration Bureau the case of Bhagat Singh Thind, whose application for naturalization had been granted in the face of the Bureau's opposition. Thind, a Caucasian of "high-caste Hindu" stock "of full Indian blood," entered the U.S. through Seattle in 1912, enrolled as a student at Berkeley in 1913, and was one of a handful of Indians who fought in World War I under the U.S. army. An article by his widow on a website that seeks to perpetuate his memory [www.bhagatsinghthind.com] states that, "upon reading Emerson, Whitman, and Thoreau, he became inspired to travel to America to fulfill his destiny as a spiritual Teacher." Thind himself denied any involvement with the Ghadr movement, though he was an unstinting advocate of Indian independence, but Judge Sutherland's decision appears not to have revolved around these considerations at all. Thind's lawyers rested their case on the two-fold argument that, on the anthropological evidence, north Indians were Aryans and thus Caucasians, and, secondly, by judicial precedent Caucasians were to be construed as whites. Justice Sutherland took the contrary view: in the "understanding of the common man," which the Court declared to be consonant with the thinking of the "original framers of the statute in 1790," "white" clearly denoted a person of European origins. "It may be true," wrote Sutherland, "that the blond Scandinavian and the brown Hindu have a common ancestor in the dim reaches of antiquity, but the average man knows perfectly well that there are unmistakable profound differences between them today." The "Aryan theory" had been "discredited by most, if not all, modern writers on the subject of ethnology," and the word "Caucasian," Sutherland argued, "is in scarcely better repute." And if all this were not enough to clinch the argument that people in "common speech" understood by the word white something quite different, or at least distinct, from Caucasian or Aryan, Sutherland held it as altogether unlikely that Congress, having opposed "Asiatic immigration generally" by the Act of February 1917, "would be willing to accept as citizens a class of persons whom it rejects as immigrants." Thus Thind, the émigré from Amritsar, was not entitled to naturalization.

Exile in the New Canaan

United States v. *Bhagat Singh Thind*, 261 U.S. 204 (1923) had, predictably, the most adverse consequences for Indian Americans. In the first instance, they ceased to be Americans. Between 1918 and 1921, the United States had denaturalized only six American citizens, all Germans. But, in the wake of the Thind decision, which had rendered Indians stateless, the Immigration Bureau and Justice Department relentlessly pursued as many Indians as they could. Though the *Nation* described it as "unthinkable that the law can be used retroactively," the Justice Department moved to rescind the American citizenship of all Indians, succeeding in doing so with some forty-five Indians over the next three years. Akhay Kumar Mozumdar, who in 1913 had been declared a full-blooded Caucasian, was ably defended by his lawyer, Sakharam Ganesh Pandit, but nonetheless became the first Indian to have his citizenship stripped from him. In due course, Pandit himself became the object of sustained government legal action. However, on March 14, 1927, more than three years after his case had first gone to court, Pandit was able to prevail when the Supreme Court refused a writ of certiorari. He had argued successfully that the court which had granted him naturalization in 1914 was acting within the law and that, contrary to the arguments of government lawyers, his naturalization was in no manner fraudulent.

Though, pursuant to the Pandit decision, the government virtually ceased to denaturalize Indians, the damage had been done. One of the most dramatic effects of the Thind decision, coupled with the Immigration Act of 1917, was the steep demographic decline of Indians. The 1940 census registered 1,476 Indians in California, a sharp drop from some 8,000 Indians estimated to be resident in California alone around 1914. Throughout the Unites States, there were only 2,045 Indians in 1940. At least 3,000 Indians were to return to their homeland between 1920 and 1940, and their story remains to be told. One other possible avenue of integration into American society had been closed to Indians when Congress passed the Cable Act in 1922. In one respect, the Cable Act, which struck down an Act of 1907 according to which a woman in the United States upon marriage automatically acquired the citizenship of her husband, appeared to be progressive. By the Act of 1907, women who were American citizens lost their citizenship if they married aliens, though they could regain their American citizenship if their husbands naturalized. The Cable Act repudiated this principle of derivative citizenship, but it made an exception insofar as it stipulated that women who married "aliens ineligible to citizenship," or Asian males, would be deprived of their U.S. citizenship. Thus Mary K. Das, who had married the Ghadrite Taraknath Das, suddenly found herself being refused an American passport in the mid-1920s.

However sustained the Indian fight to gain rights of citizenship, by far the greatest impact of the Thind decision and the legislative measures of the previous years was in the domain of land ownership. The State Commission of Immigration and Housing had in 1920 noted that "Hindus in California are generally employed in agricultural pursuits," and that many Hindus had moved rapidly from the ranks of the employed to the ranks of employers and thus become "little landlord[s]." Punjabis had an enviable reputation as farmers, and at least a few in the Sacramento and Imperial Valleys, which together accounted for about 90 percent of all the land farmed by Indians, had established mini-empires. Jawala Singh came to be known as the "Potato King." California newspapers, such as the *San Francisco Chronicle* and the *Fresno Morning Republican*, rejoiced at the Thind ruling and openly suggested that much work remained to be done to diminish what they falsely projected as the growing economic affluence of Indians. At least one newspaper, the *Sacramento Bee*, opined in an editorial in March 1923 that the decision of the Supreme Court, "that Hindus are not eligible to American citizenship, is most welcome in California;" but it also urged that "Hindu holders of land" be brought "within the mandatory provisions of the California anti-alien land law. There must be no more leasing or sale of land to such immigrants from India." California Attorney General U.S. Webb indicated that he would seek the rigorous application of the Alien Land Law (1913, amended 1920–1921), which prevented non-citizens from owning and leasing land, to Indians.

Indians took recourse to various measures and subterfuges in an effort to retain possession of their lands and businesses. The brothers Johnny Khan and Kalu Khan who had acquired property in 1919 in Butte County to the northwest of Sacramento managed to retain control over their land over the next twenty years by "conveying the land from time to time to third persons, taking back fictitious notes, mortgages and deed of trust, thus lending a semblance of validity to their possession, use and ownership of land." One common response was to transfer land into the hands of friendly Anglo farmers and business associates. The transfer itself could take various forms, entailing, for instance, a nominal payment to the caretaker, or the creation of a dummy partnership whereby land was actually purchased in the name of an American citizen. There are cases where the "friendly" or "silent" partner appropriated the land, or insisted on a handsome payment for its return. The most successful strategy was to place the land in the names of American-born children, but many Indian men could not resort to this expedient as they remained unmarried or had wives who been left behind in India. Women accounted for much less than one percent of all Indians in 1914, and men who might have contemplated going back to India to fetch a bride could not do so after 1917 when they and their wives would have been barred from entering the United States. Some Indians responded to the changed circumstances with the dogged determination to prove that they were, in the words of a bill unsuccessfully introduced in the House of Representatives to grant citizenship to Indians who had been in the U.S. prior to 1924, "of pure Aryan blood." The Punjabis, especially, construed themselves "as pure Caucasians"—as much "as the Germans." The outcome was occasionally tragic: Vaisho Das Bagai, who had immigrated to the U.S. in 1915, and become a naturalized citizen, committed suicide in 1928. The note he left at his death stated that he had tried to become "as American as possible."

The Immigration (National Origins Quota) Act of 1924 barred any "alien ineligible for citizenship" from immigration to the United States and thus shut out all Asians except Filipinos. This, at least, is what we might term the official history of Indians in the U.S., but what is equally known from history is the fact that borders are notoriously difficult to enforce. Every age has had its own strand of "illegal" immigration and there has never been a time when undocumented workers have not furnished a labor force that employers were eager to utilize and exploit. Rozina Visram and, more recently, Michael Fisher have both documented the presence of an Indian lascar subculture in Britain dating back to the late 1700s, and evidence points to a similar history at a later period on the East Coast of the United States. Britain's domination of international shipping paved the way for Indian seamen to travel around the world on board British ships, working as waiters, stewards, cooks, and furnace men. Scattered articles in the *New York Times* from 1907 onwards point to the arrival of Indian lascars in increasing numbers over subsequent years, though how many stayed behind, melting into the population, making their home in tenements on the lower East Side, and even forging sexual and marriage alliances with black and Puerto Rican women is not yet known. That their numbers may not have been inconsiderable is suggested by revealing *New York Times* articles in July 1922. On the 9th, the headlines stated: "Rail Shop Strike at Deadlock Here. . . .Tension in Jersey City. Further Disorders Feared as Result of Presence of Negro and Hindu Workers." The article that appeared on July 12 began, "Strikers Migrate to Take Rail Jobs," with further subheadlines pointing to some excitement in the general population at a large influx of Hindus and Chinese: "Asiatics Stir Jersey City." The Eerie Railroad, the newspaper reported, had hired as strike-breakers "fifty Hindus and thirty-one Chinese" whom it described as having deserted their ships at port. On account of "dull shipping," the article states, some "5000 Chinese and Hindus [were] stranded in this port." Some of these lascars would have returned with their ships; others slipped into the city, found lodgings at workingmen's homes and boarding-houses, and took up jobs as cooks and factory workers. Their history has not so far been told.

On the West Coast, similarly, one has to make allowance for some illegal Indian immigration into the United States from Mexico. Nonetheless, it cannot be doubted that the Indian community rapidly diminished in size in the two decades after the Thind decision. For the Indians who stayed behind, it became necessary to innovate and adapt to their social conditions. California legislation of 1881 forbade marriages of Chinese with whites, and over the years the antimiscegenation laws made marriages between whites and virtually all other Asians nearly impossible. In California, at least, Indian men would have encountered Mexican women, and social and sexual liaisons developed between them even before the Cable Act of 1922 and the calamitous Thind decision of the following year. "There have already been quite a few marriages," Taraknath Das observed in 1923, "between Mexican women and Hindustani men." Though Mexicans were technically classified as "white," we should recall Justice Sutherland's opinion that in the "popular sense" of the term, white was understood to be white Europeans. Certainly no one in the white community had any strenuous objections to mixed Mexican-Indian marriages. Court clerks applied their own discretion, as the marriage of one Sher Singh of Holtville, Imperial Valley, in 1916 to a Mexican woman demonstrates. "While in doubt as to their legal right to marry under the laws of the state," the clerk nonetheless issued the license, "thereby passing the responsibility up to any authorized person who performs the marriage ceremony." The social anthropologist Karen Leonard, whose ethnography of California's Punjabi Mexican Americans has shed much light on this community, has underscored the arbitrariness of the classifications with a brilliant example of a second-generation Punjabi Mexican woman. When she went to the hospital in 1958 to deliver a baby, she was labeled "Hindu;" at the birth of her second and third children, in 1959 and 1960, she was listed as "Mexican-Hindu" and "white," respectively.

Adapting themselves to differences in language, cuisine, dress, and religion, Punjabi men and Mexican women together created an unusual bi-ethnic community. Their common brown—or, in the language of Benjamin Franklin, "tawney"—color apart, both had labored on farms. The subaltern status of each community in relation to the dominant white society would have been all too obvious, though what might have impelled Mexican women to marry Punjabi men is far from clear. It is also necessary to stress what is equally obvious but seldom mentioned, namely that the history of Punjabi Mexican Americans occupies a significant place in the narrative of the Indian diaspora in the United States but a comparatively minor place in the history of Mexican Americans. The supposed similarity of Mexican and Indian culture has been stressed by some commentators: tortillas are to rotis or chapattis what jalapeno peppers are to chilies. A much later generation of Indian Americans, inspired by Third Worldism and the idea of non-alignment in a highly polarized world, waxed eloquent about Mexico, and at least one writer's observations in 1974 suggest something of what Indians in the United States might have experienced even in the first half of the twentieth century: "For Indians, Mexico is the only country that provides all that is missing in the Western hemisphere. People are warm and friendly. They eat the same sort of food with lots of spices and, above all, they have a sense of respect concerning anything related to India. Here there is no color bar. Mexicans look so much like Indians that there is no possibility of racial discrimination " (*India Abroad*, October 4, 1974). The great Mexican poet, and former ambassador of Mexico to India, Octavio Paz, would come to much the same conclusion about what we might describe as the cultural and emotional proximity of Mexico to India. Not by the crucial presence of chilis in both cuisines, but also by their shared experiments in anti-colonial nation-making, does Paz describe the "Antipodes of Coming and Going" in characterizing the intertwined histories of Mexico and India.

Nevertheless, as Leonard and other scholars have documented, Punjabi-Mexican marriages proved extraordinarily difficult to sustain. At a time, from the late 1910s to the 1950s, when divorce was comparatively uncommon, and even more infrequent in rural, foreign-born communities, nearly a third of the Punjabi-Mexican marriages ended in divorce; significantly, the women filed for divorce as often did the men. The women complained that their husbands had been adulterous, while the men charged their wives with desertion and dereliction of duty. More than one contemporary observer noted that Punjabi men were rather too fond of their liquor and often got into drunken brawls. To be sure, as Leonard argues, there were some happy marriages—but here Tolstoy's adage, "All happy families are alike, but unhappy marriages are unhappy in their own way," suggests why a social narrative of happy Mexican-Punjabi marriages remains elusive. The singular fact remains that Punjabi men who wished to marry and remain in the United States had no other recourse but to wed Mexican women. One early immigrant, Nihal Singh, may not quite have had a premonition of things to come, but his article in *Out West* in 1909 put the matter quite dramatically: "There is only one Hindoo woman on the North American continent. She lives with her husband, a doctor of Vedic medicine, in Vancouver, B.C."

The social decline of the Indian community in the decades following the early 1920s matched the demographic debacle. The 1940 census, which counted 2,045 Indians throughout the

United States, offered a dim portrait of a rapidly aging community where 56 percent of the people were over forty years of age. It revealed that only 4 percent of the Indians were professionals, and some 70 percent were employed as laborers, over two-thirds of them on farms. If today Indian Americans send more of their young women and men to college than any other community, one is sobered by the thought that in 1940 Indians had the lowest educational accomplishments of any ethnic group. Of the Indians twenty-five years and older, some 40 percent had not completed even one year of schooling. This community was beginning to resemble the diasporic Indian communities of Trinidad and Fiji, insofar as direct ties with India had greatly diminished. Among Indian visitors to the United States, if one might consider the perspective from the other side, the perception that the United States had become supremely inhospitable to Asians was widespread. This perception is perhaps nowhere registered so forcefully as in the story of Nobel Laureate Rabindranath Tagore's despair at the racism that he experienced in Los Angeles on a visit in 1929. He then wrote, "Jesus could not get into America because, first of all, He would not have the necessary money, and secondly, He would be an Asiatic."

The 1930s have generally been written off in histories of Indian Americans as a period of despair and inactivity, but Indian Americans activists, educators, and intellectuals were laying the groundwork for a sustained campaign both to restore citizenship rights for Indians and to secure American support in India's fight for independence from British rule. Taraknath Das, whom we have previously encountered as one of the principal figures in the Ghadr movement and an advocate of the rights of Indians, also assumed some importance as an educator and interlocutor between India and the United States. He was joined by a galaxy of other figures, most prominently among them Rajani Kanta Das, Haridas Mazumdar, Dhan Gopal Mukerji, Krishnalal Sridharani, and Sudhindra Bose. Though it would be something of a stretch to describe them as having played a critical or even important role in giving shape to Indian studies at American universities, they endeavored to place before the

American public an account of Indian society and politics not filtered by British colonialism. Rajani Kanta Das earned his PhD in economics from the University of Chicago in 1915, taught at New York University, and authored nearly a dozen books on Indian labor which emerged in a steady stream from the early 1920s onwards. His books on *Labor Legislation in India* (1930), *Plantation Labor in India* (1931), *History of Indian Labor Legislation* (1941), and *Wartime Labor Conditions in India* (1945) established him as an authority in labor studies.

Dhan Gopal Mukerji (1890–1936) was brought up to be a priest in Bengal, but he left for Japan in 1909 and then made his way to California, where he earned degrees at Berkeley and Stanford. Over his short life, he authored nearly two dozen books, including many that became children's classics. His *Caste and Outcaste* (1923) was immensely popular, went through five editions in a few years, and was translated into several European languages. While the first half of the book aimed to give an "intimate expression of Eastern life" for American audiences, the second half provided a description of his life as a student, laborer, and farmer in the United States. Mukerji eulogized Hindu civilization, viewing it as the cradle of tolerance and pluralism. While the discrimination he had experienced in the U.S. made him less receptive to grandiose claims about America's alleged love affair with freedom, his views of the Islamic phase of Indian history certainly appear to have been colored by British colonial narratives. Nevertheless, as the scholar Gordon Chang has quite recently argued, Mukerji has perhaps the "distinction of being the first author of Asian Indian ancestry who successfully wrote for American audiences about Indian life." Mukerji is the first Indian in the U.S. to have made his mark as what used to be called a "man of letters," and he appears to have earned his livelihood through writing. He committed suicide in his New York apartment in 1936.

The mid-1920s to the early 1940s were, in another critical respect, more fruitful than has been imagined. The Reverend John Haynes Holmes, an American Minister, had proclaimed Gandhi in a widely hailed sermon as "the greatest man in the world" in the early 1920s, and thereafter many Christian preachers and missionaries confessed that, even though Gandhi was not a Christian, he bore more of a similarity to Christ than any living Christian. Gandhi may not then have been a household name in the United States, but he still had a considerable following among liberals, pacifists, intellectuals, and some clergymen. Gandhi's famous march to the sea in 1930, captured on film by a number of American journalists, catapulted him on to the world stage, nor was this merely a matter of fifteen minutes of fame. From then until his assassination on January 30, 1948, he had a constant stream of visitors from the United States, and the African American press, which had championed the noncooperation movement (1920–1922) and the civil disobedience campaign (1930–1931), played a critical role in inspiring African American leaders, activists, and intellectuals—among them, Howard Thurman, Sue Bailey Thurman, Benjamin E. Mays, Mordecai Johnson, Channing Tobia, Bayard Rustin, William Stuart Nelson—to visit Gandhi in India. His fasts and terms of imprisonment were immense sources of consternation, just as the entire gamut of his political activities received incessant media coverage.

Not surprisingly, a number of Indians in the United States also saw themselves as his spokesmen. Haridas Mazumdar, who had arrived in the U.S. as a student, earning a doctorate in sociology from the University of Wisconsin in 1929, became one of Gandhi's most ardent champions. Over four decades he published several books on Gandhi, including *Gandhi the Apostle*: *His Trial and His Message* (1923), *Gandhi versus the Empire* (1932), and *Gandhi as an Educationist* (1935). In Krishnalal Sridharani, Gandhi had an eloquent and sophisticated spokesperson, even an influential theorist whose *War Without Violence* (1939) provided a strategic framework for nonviolent political action. He followed this up with *Warning to the West* (1942) and *The Mahatma and the World* (1946), but *My India, My America*, a gigantic memoir, is more illustrative of the sensibility of a person who saw himself as genuinely bicultural.

Sridharani, Mazumdar, and others did not only consolidate Gandhi's reputation in the U.S. They suggested that while Gandhi belonged to the world, the fact that he had, as Jawaharlal Nehru would put it at a later date, become synonymous with India could not be overlooked. Gandhi's Indian American proponents worked on the intuition that his name was calculated to earn India prestige and provide India with a reservoir of goodwill upon which the country could draw from time to time. Los Angeles-based engineer, businessman, and educational philanthropist Navin Doshi recalls that when he came to the United States as a student in the 1950s, "people used to respect us because we came from Gandhi's country. . . . The opportunities we Indians got in this country are due to the high esteem in which Americans held Gandhi. The first generation capitalized on that goodwill and built a reputation for Indians. The current generation is cashing in on that reputation." If in the early 1960s Martin Luther King could say that to other countries he went as a tourist but that he had come to India alone as a pilgrim and disciple of Gandhi, in no small measure the origins of this sentiment can be traced back to the work done by Indian Americans in contributing to the enhanced reputation of Gandhi as a world figure.

By the mid to late 1930s, Indian Americans felt well positioned to seek political changes through institutional frameworks. The India Welfare League, headed by Mubarak Ali Khan, and the India League of America, founded by the charismatic merchant and lobbyist Sirdar Jagjit Singh in 1938, renewed efforts to obtain citizenship for Indians and increase American support for Indian demands for independence from British rule. Not everyone held out the hope that Congress would take action to restore naturalization rights for Indians, and Khairata Ram Samras filed a petition in a San Francisco court seeking the overthrow of the Thind decision of 1923. These challenges may also have been precipitated by the recognition that the Indian community had experienced a dramatic demographic decline, and that the community was, perhaps, on the verge of extinction—an outcome that might well have transpired but for the altered circumstances arising out of World War II. By the late 1930s, the Roosevelt administration was already contemplating a scenario where India might be asked to assist China in the war with Japan. The joint issuance by Winston Churchill and Franklin Roosevelt in 1941 of the Atlantic Charter, which recognized the right of all peoples to self-government, as well as the growing American perception that Indian assistance in the war might be critical in preventing the formation of a Japanese-German military axis in Asia, were both conducive in advancing the claims of Asian Indians. "America cannot afford to say that she wants the people of India to fight on her side," wrote the Asian Indian demographer S. Chandrasekhar, "and at the same time maintain that she will not have them among her immigrant groups." That was not, however, the only difficulty. Churchill remained an implacable foe of Indian independence, and Gandhi and other leaders of the Indian National Congress, also acutely aware that the Atlantic Charter was (as Walter Benjamin would have said) another "document of civilization" that the West would flaunt before the world, were adamant in holding to the view that their support of the war could only be obtained if Britain was fully committed to Indian independence. That Roosevelt was susceptible to Churchill's views on India is nowhere better demonstrated than in his acquiescence to the British arrest of Gandhi in August 1942 and the severe crackdown on the "Quit India" movement that Gandhi had launched. Nevertheless, the swift Japanese occupation of Southeast Asia must certainly have played a part in persuading Roosevelt's administration both to support Indian independence and naturalization rights for Indians in the United States.

The untiring efforts of Sirdar Jagjit Singh and others would lead in March 1944 to the introduction of bills, sponsored by New York Congressman Emmanuel Cellar and Connecticut Congresswoman Clare Booth Luce, providing for naturalization of Indians and a quota for Indian immigrants. Jagjit Singh, or "JJ" as he was known, set into operation a formidable lobbying machinery that he had assiduously put into place through the cultivation of influential people and the creation of networks. He used his close friendship, and possibly sexual intimacy, with Clare Luce, the wife of publisher Henry Luce, to press for less hostile coverage of Indian nationalism in *Time*'s pages. Not for nothing, JJ realized, had more than one American philosopher described business as the business of America. If, in other words, American politicians could be persuaded that India was a logical target for the expansion of American business interests, they would be much more inclined to remove the legal disabilities under which Indian Americans suffered. JJ's testimony before Congress in early 1945 bears an uncanny resemblance to the arguments that have been advanced in recent years for closer ties between India and the United States and greater American investment in a country now more receptive to neoliberalization policies. "The 400 million East Indians," JJ reminded Congress, "represent great untapped trade reservoir. There exists over there a great demand for American goods." JJ was, of course, far from being the only one to agitate for conferral of immigration and naturalization rights for Indians. Jawaharlal Nehru's charismatic sister, Vijayalakshmi Pandit, arrived in 1945 and made an eloquent case for Indian independence in well-attended talks around the country. In California, Dalip Singh Saund, who had arrived at Berkeley from a small village in the Punjab, found that an Indian with a doctorate in mathematics had no employment prospects. Saund, who wrote in his 1960 autobiography of how he had made America his home even when the country had not accepted him, took to farming and politics, and criss-crossed the country stirring up support for Indians as the first President of the India Association of America (founded 1942).

The Luce-Cellar (Immigration) Act of 1946, or Public Law 483, signed into law on July 2nd by President Truman, not only conferred on Indians the right to naturalization but also set an annual quota of one hundred immigrants from India. Since this triumphal moment has achieved a hagiographic status in Indian recollections of their struggle to achieve equality in the United States, it is a political imperative to recall that even the advocates of the legislation, such as Clare Booth Luce, supported it not from any intrinsic belief in the equality of colored people and white Americans but because failure to pass the bill would erode America's "moral leadership not only throughout the Asiatic world, but here at home among our own colored people." Mrs. Luce described herself as the "first to protest against people of any nation, of any color, coming here in such numbers as to lower our living standards and weaken our culture. This is a principle on which we are all agreed. And it does so happen that the peoples of the Orient can underlive us." It was absolutely necessary, Mrs. Luce remarked, to keep "Oriental immigration" greatly restricted, but keeping "orientals" out of the U.S. altogether was "certainly improper." The "generosity" in allowing one hundred Indians entry into the United States annually could not have been lost on them, only eighteen of whom were admitted in the first year.

Between 1948 and 1965, 7,000 Indians were to immigrate to the United States, and nearly 1,780 Indians, many who had been American residents for two decades or more, acquired American citizenship. Three years after the passage of the Immigration Act, Saund fulfilled his aspiration to be an American citizen, and immediately thereafter won a seat, which he had to give up as he not been a citizen for one year, as judge in Westmoreland Judicial District. His political experience stood him in good stead: Saund ran a successful campaign to get elected to Congress in 1956, the first Asian American to achieve this distinction, and served three two-year terms in the House of Representatives. Meanwhile, after a long spell in India, Jagjit Singh returned to the United States, and at the 1960 session of the UN General Assembly he pushed for a resolution condemning the Chinese occupation of Tibet. He then, from 1961 to 1964, served as national chairman of the U.S. Committee for the United Nations. For the time being, the political struggle, in the narrowest sense of the term, had ended; as Indian professionals would begin to populate the United States, before long they found that another struggle had to be waged at the workplace.

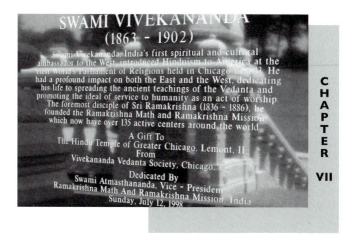

Emergence of a Diasporic Community

The present phase of the history of Indian Americans in the United States begins with the National Origins Act of 1965. The McCarran-Walter Immigration Nationality Act of 1952 had repealed the Barred Zone Act of 1917, and the Alien Land Law was similarly declared unconstitutional (*Fuji Sei* v. *State of California*), but immigration from Asian countries was still highly restricted. President Kennedy had added his voice to those of many others who felt that restrictive policies were impeding America's capacity to compete worldwide for the best scientific talent. Some Americans feared that "communist propaganda" would succeed in persuading the world that the United States was at its core a profoundly racist nation, and neither the miniscule quotas placed on Asian migration nor, even more significantly, the virulence with which black civil rights activists had been attacked were facts that did America proud. The Civil Rights Act of 1964 necessitated immediate immigration reform, and the 1965 INS legislation devised immigrant visas according to seven preferential categories and set a quota of 20,000 for each country in the "Eastern Hemisphere," though most immediate family members of U.S. citizens were not subject to numeric limits. This system of immigration, with some modifications, such as the abandonment of the hemispheric quotas, is still largely in place. The greater number of Indians, at least in the first fifteen years, was to arrive as professionals, and the 1975 census revealed that an astonishing 93 percent were classified as "professional/technical workers." More than anything else, they thought principally of their economic and professional advancement; with the passage of time, and as they settled down, family reunification became a prime consideration. By 1975 the number of Asian Indians had risen to well over 175,000; and it is around this time that the question of self-representation, or how they wished to be known collectively to others, first surfaced among members of the Indian community.

Maxine P. Fisher, who in 1980 published a study of Asian Indians in New York City, the first monograph of its kind, reported that her informants variously described themselves as Aryan, Indo-Aryan, Caucasian, Oriental, Indian, Asian, Mongol, and Dravidian, and she implied that as Indians could be "very fair," "very dark," or anywhere in the "middle," race and skin color had no necessary association. The earlier and quaint nomenclature of "Hindus" to designate everyone from the Indian subcontinent had long been abandoned, and the birth of Pakistan in 1947 signified that no longer were all South Asians Indians. (There were much fewer Sri Lankans or Nepalese in the U.S. at that time, and insofar as the term "South Asia" was ever used, it was understood to refer to the Indian subcontinent.) But the designation of "Indians" was scarcely more acceptable, since what are now known as "Native Americans" were also known as "Indians." The confusion between "Red Indians" and "Indians" might sound absurd, but as a satirical scene in Mira Nair's popular film, *Mississippi Masala*, suggests, to the mind of some Americans at least this confusion was real. The term "Asian American" was not much in vogue, largely referencing those from the Far East (and later Southeast Asia); and, unlike in Britain, where Indians perhaps tolerated being lumped alongside Africans and Caribbean people under the generic category of "black," even deriving new political coalitions and formations in the common interest of combating oppression, in the United States the designation "black" was seen as condemning one to membership in a permanent underclass. Some scholars and commentators have suggested the term "desis," now quite in vogue among certain (mostly chic) class of Indian Americans, but there is nothing to show that the term, which in Hindi means "local," "indigenous," of one's own hometown rather than from abroad ("videshi"), was in use around the late 1970s.

The Census of 1980 placed the number of Indian Americans at 387,223. In ten years, their population had grown some thirty-fold, but Korean, Chinese, Filipino, and Vietnamese immigration had also grown by leaps and bounds. Efforts were afoot among Indians to preserve their minority status and bore fruit when the Census Bureau agreed, with effect from 1980, to reclassify immigrants from India as "Asian Indians." By this time, some of the demographic patterns which continue to characterize the Indian community to the present day were reasonably well-established. Unlike other Asian ethnic groups, which are to be found in disproportionately large numbers on the West Coast, the Indian population is more evenly distributed throughout the United States. California had, in 1920, accounted for nearly 70 percent of the Indian population, a figure which dropped to 15 percent in 1980, and rose to 29 percent in 1990. There has been for many years a heavy density of Indians in the northeast, particularly in the New York–New Jersey area, but the 1990 census shows that large Indian communities had emerged in Chicago and its western suburbs, the Bay Area in northern California, and in southern California around Los Angeles and Orange County. Secondly, more so than other ethnic groups, Indians have largely gravitated towards urban areas, a pattern confirmed by the 2000 census, which shows significant Indian communities, besides those enumerated above, in the Washington, DC area (over 50,000 Indians) and in the urban belts of Texas, where Indians are now the third largest Asian American group after the Vietnamese and Chinese. Thirdly, the exponential growth of the Asian Indian community shows no sign of abatement. Between 1980 and 1990, the annual growth rate of the community was 8.5 percent. Nearly half-million Indians were added to take their number to over 815,000. From 1990 to 2000, the Indian population again more than doubled to 1.71 million, by far the greatest jump for any large Asian American ethnic group. Among large immigrant communities from which 35,000 or more immigrants were being admitted annually to the U.S. in the mid-1990s, Indians overtook Dominicans, the Chinese, and Vietnamese by 1996 by substantial margins, registering a growth rate exceeded only by Mexican immigrants. Constituting 16.4 percent of the Asian American population, the Asian Indian community is today exceeded in size only by the Filipinos (18 percent) and Chinese (23 percent).

Fourthly, the educational attainment level of Asian Indians continues to be very high, though the percentage of those who earn their living as professionals has declined. Across all groups, according to the 2000 census, 24.4 percent of Americans had earned at least a bachelor's degree; however, among all Asian Americans the figure rises to 44.1 percent, and to an astounding 63.9 percent among Asian Indians. A third of all Indians have one or more advanced degrees, a much higher figure than for any other ethnic or racial group. The Educational Testing Service (ETS), which administers standardized exams, in a report on Asian American students in 1997 found that the percentage of South Asian high school seniors who scored above the fiftieth percentile in reading was substantially higher than all other Asian American communities and between 4 to 11 percentage points higher in mathematics in comparison to Koreans, Chinese, and Japanese who are their closest competitors. The argument that Indian Americans are attuned to English from a younger age than other Asian Americans is entirely plausible, particularly if we keep in mind the migration of professional Indians, the vast majority of whom had their education in India in the English language, though how far this argument can be extended to second generation Asian Americans is much more uncertain.

One can turn, as well, to very different kinds of indices to gauge the educational levels of Asian Americans. Between May 1998 and July 1999, the U.S. government issued 134,000 new H-1B visas, which are granted for a period of six years to highly skilled foreigners seeking employment in the United States. 63,900 of these visas were granted to Indians alone. Ordinarily, 85,000 H-1B visas are granted annually, 20,000 of these to holders of advanced degrees, and Indians account for a minimum of 36 percent of these visas. By 2003, according to reliable estimates, a total of some 400,000 Asian Indians were holders of H-1B visas. Though the H-1B is not an immigrant visa, and its holder is viewed as an "alien," typically a very large percentage of H-1B visa holders eventually acquire permanent residency. But even among permanent residents and citizens, the continued preponderance of Indian professionals is easily estimated by a survey of doctors, engineers, and computer specialists. The prestigious Indian Institutes of Technology (at Kharagpur, Kanpur, Chennai, Mumbai, Delhi, and much more recently at Guwahati and Roorkee) have sent as much as 40 percent of their graduating class in some years to the United States, and nearly 23,000 IIT graduates are estimated to have made the U.S. their home. Constituting about 0.6 percent of the U.S. population, Asian Indian students typically account for between 5 to 10 percent of major awards, such as Presidential Scholarships, Intel Science Talent Search awards, and the like. For 2007, four of the thirty-two American students who have been named Rhodes Scholars are of Indian origin.

Such broad demographic and sociological patterns may disguise as much as they reveal, apart from the fact that they say little about the politics of this category, "Asian Indian." As we have seen, Indians had attempted at one point to be assimilated into the category of "white" or "Caucasian." In the 1970s, however, claiming to be white was a scarcely desirable political strategy, and not only because it meant disowning the civil rights movement and the gains that African Americans had won, even though not everyone recognized the movement for what it was, for *all* minorities. Whereas minorities were at one time subjected to open discrimination, fifty years after the Thind decision the designation of "minority" was also calculated to earn one certain entitlements, whatever prejudices might still exist against minorities. Writing to the U.S. Civil Rights Commission in 1975, the recently formed Association of Indians in America (AIA) submitted that, keeping in mind that the Civil Rights Act aimed at protecting the rights of individuals who were also discriminated against on the basis of appearance, it was undeniably true that "Indians are different in appearance; they are equally dark-skinned as other non-white individuals and are, therefore, subject to the same prejudices." The admission that Indians could be "equally dark-skinned" as other non-whites is not one that Indians would readily have made to each other, and the anecdotal evidence that Indian Americans were keen to be distanced from African Americans is much too strong to ignore.

However opportunistic the position of the AIA, there was something of a case to be made for disadvantages suffered by Indians, for as the 1980 census showed, U.S.-born Asian Indians, whose numbers were very small but growing, had an unemployment rate "five times that of other Asian American groups." A comprehensive study conducted by the University of California, the results of which appeared in the *Pacific Rim States Asian Demographic Data Book*, suggested that fifteen years later large pockets of poverty still persisted among Indian Americans in California. In 1995, the mean per capita household income of Indians in California was $18,472, below the $20,676 per capita income of the population as a whole and more than $3,000 below the per capita income of white Americans. A report released in March 2005, *The Diverse Face of Asians and Pacific Islanders in California*, still bears out the earlier findings: 14 percent of Indian Americans in the Central Valley, where agricultural work predominates, are living below the poverty level, 39 percent have little or no proficiency in English, and 35 percent have failed to earn a high school diploma. Strikingly, while the idea of India remained synonymous with poverty for many Americans, and at dinner tables American children were told that they were not to waste food while millions of children in India went to bed most nights on an empty stomach, the idea of poverty among Indian Americans would have struck most Americans as anomalous.

Today, considering the general affluence of the Indian American community, the idea that is just as likely to persist among Americans is that India is doing well. Indeed, considering the proliferation of news items about the explosive growth of the Indian economy, some people have gained the impression, which is far from being even remotely accurate, that most people in India are wealthy. I recall a conversation last year at Sam Woo's BBQ, a popular restaurant serving Cantonese food in the San Fernando Valley, where one of the waiters told me that he thought of Indians everywhere as generally well-to-do. The reports on poverty among Indians in the Central Valley in California belie the more frequently encountered image of Asian Indians as people who are invariably well-educated and placed in professional positions—in the same state of California, well more than 25 percent of the 2000 dotcom businesses in Silicon Valley in 1999 were started by Indians. In most years during the last decade, Indians have accounted for about 20 percent of the startups in Silicon Valley. The foreign-born population of San Jose in 1970 was 7.6 percent; in the 2000 Census, this figure had gone up to 26.8 percent. Indians are far from being the only foreign-born arrivals in San Jose or Santa Clara County in the heart of Silicon Valley, and, in whole numbers, they are outnumbered by the Chinese, whose achievements have not been any less spectacular. But what makes the success of Indians all the more remarkable is that they have been late arrivals. AnnaLee Saxenian's painstaking work on immigrant entrepreneurship in Silicon Valley around 1990 reveals that 71 percent of the Chinese and 87 percent of the Indians employed in high-technology industries arrived in the United States after 1970; for 1980, the corresponding figures are 41 percent and 60 percent, respectively.

Though the fact of the ascendancy of Indian professionals is now widely recognized, their narrative remains woefully incomplete. Stories about racism, discrimination, and the "glass ceiling" are frequently encountered in conversations, but little empirical work has been done among engineers, math and computer scientists, natural scientists, and those in the health professions to document such stories. Saxenian's aforementioned study of immigrant professionals notes that few Chinese and Indians have attained managerial positions in Silicon Valley, but she avers that "income data provide little support for the glass ceiling hypothesis." Yet, as she maintains, two-thirds of Asian professionals believe that their professional advancement to managerial positions is limited by race, and that "these concerns increased significantly with the age and experience of the respondents." She admits that this "perception is consistent with the finding that in [the] technology industry at least, Chinese and Indians remain concentrated in professional rather than managerial positions, despite superior levels of educational attainment."

An Indian engineer who arrived in the U.S. four decades ago for his doctorate and in recent years has moved to the very top of his profession, acting as the president of a professional organization with nearly 100,000 members, has shared with me his insights into the difficulties that were once encountered by Indian professionals but, he claims, are much less frequently witnessed these days. As he explained to me, racism took comparatively subtle forms: Indians who thought that their qualifications, experience, and accomplishments entitled them to senior positions were told that they were not sufficiently well-informed about "American culture" to assume leadership positions, or that their own cultural upbringing precluded them from exercising effective leadership; at other times, it was hinted that they had good written skills but were deficient in oral communication. Another second-generation Indian American woman, who was born in the United States and has recently finished a doctorate, tells me that she has had sustained conversations with her father who came to the United States around 1970 and did very well for himself as an engineer after earning his Ph.D. from a leading American university. However, she claims, he has been reluctant to admit that obstacles were placed in the way of his advancement; indeed, it was a mark of honor, partly as a mark of gratitude to a country which had done so much for an immigrant, to pretend that setbacks to one's career all arose from one's own shortcomings. Very recently, he has been offered the second highest managerial position in one of the world's most well-known IT companies, but that company is now headed by an Indian, and the negotiations were all conducted with other senior Indian managers in that firm.

There seems to be, indeed, a general consensus among Indian American professionals of the first generation that few Indians were ever promoted to senior managerial positions, and one suspects that fifteen years after the INS Act of 1965, an organization such as the Association of Indians in America (AIA) had already been brought to the awareness that some representation of Indians was necessary to advance their interests. At another level, when AIA in the late 1970s commenced its agitation to have Indian Americans declared a distinct minority, it was also contending with the reality that with every passing year the number of Indians employed as taxi drivers, gas station owners and attendants, subway news agent vendors, and in other working-class jobs was growing. Moreover, the apprehension that Indian Americans, whose success also rendered them vulnerable, might soon have to bear the brunt of racial prejudice and ethnic jokes was not entirely misplaced. In the mid-1980s, this racism acquired a systematic patterning: thus, in New Jersey, a number of Indians were violently attacked by young white men who flamboyantly described themselves as "dotbusters, the dot a reference to the *bindi* placed by some Hindu women on their forehead between the eyebrows. Indian businesses were vandalized; women were molested; and thirty-year old Citicorp executive Navroze Mody was bludgeoned to death.

Among Indian professionals, then, the sense that the discrimination which every immigrant group experiences for a generation or two might stare them in the face began to acquire some urgency in the early 1980s. As the laws governing the admission of doctors from overseas into the American medical profession were tightened, the American Association of Physicians of Indian Origin (AAPI) was formed to represent this constituency. There has since been an astronomical increase in the number of Indian American doctors. According to an estimate furnished in 1993, Indian doctors constituted 4 percent of all doctors in the United States, thereby forming the largest ethnic group of doctors in the country; and the high profile of AAPI, which established a permanent legislative office in Washington, DC in December 1995 and keeps track of Indian doctors by their Congressional district, can be gauged by the fact that its annual convention the same year was addressed by President Bill Clinton, and that in other years speakers have included Vice President Dan Quayle, Speaker Newt Gingrich, and House Minority Leader Richard Gephardt. AAPI today has 130 chapters, and it "represents" at least 42,000 physicians of Indian origin working in the United States. Its web site, www.aapiusa.org, predictably positions Indians both as the inheritors of a great medical tradition, stretching back to the practitioners Atreya and Susruta, working in 600 BC or "nearly 150 years before Hippocrates," and as something of a vanguard working in a country which itself has stretched the frontiers of medical research. "Although Asian Indians constitute less than 1 percent of the population in the United States," the web site reminds readers, "they constitute 10-12 percent of the student body in medical schools in the U.S. This dynamic, bright, and enthusiastic group are our future."

Other broader-based organizations also emerged to enhance and safeguard Indian interests. Their history is considerably fragmented, and not all of it is germane to an understanding of the involvement of Indian Americans in contemporary politics. By the early 1970s, there seem to have been over a dozen organizations in the New York area. The Joint Committee of Indian Organizations was founded in 1971, and it helped initiate celebrations to mark both American holidays as well as the most important national Indian holidays, such as Republic Day (January 30th), Independence Day (August 15th), and Gandhi's Birthday (October 2nd). The Federation of Indian Associations (New York) grew out of the Joint Committee in 1978, and in the following year it successfully campaigned, along with other Asian American organizations, to have the first week of May proclaimed annually across the nation as Asian American week. Before long chapters had been established in Chicago, Los Angeles, Philadelphia, San Francisco,

Washington, and elsewhere, and they were all brought under the rubric of the National Federation of Indian American Associations (NFIA), which could now claim to represent Indians across the country. The NFIA, together with the Indian American Forum for Political Education (IAFPE), founded in 1982 to help Indians get elected to local and national office and bring them into the mainstream of political activity, and AAPI (Association of American Physicians of Indian Origin), agitated against proposed legislation in 1985 that would have deeply cut Medicare funding to hospitals employing doctors with foreign medical degrees. Among its other principal political achievements, NFIA lobbied in the early years, alongside other Asian American organizations, to defeat a Congressional bill that would have drastically reduced the number of relatives allowed into the U.S. under the second and fifth preference categories for, respectively, adult unmarried children and married siblings.

In assessing the activities of more politically minded Indian organizations, we should well remember that their members worked on the assumption that the advancement of Indians in the United States was intrinsically related to India's standing in the world, the country's economic progress, and its geopolitical alliances. If India remained poverty-stricken, "under-developed," hostile to foreign investments, and indisposed towards the United States politically, Indian Americans were unlikely to create a favorable impression on American politicians. India's advocacy of non-alignment under Nehru, and the subsequent treaty of friendship with the Soviet Union, won India virtually no friends in successive American administrations, and Indian Americans likewise found themselves bereft of any benefactors or even listeners in Washington. However, by the mid-1980s, the groundwork for a closer relationship between India and the U.S. was laid with a state visit to Washington by then Prime Minister Rajiv Gandhi. NFIA would then show how Indian Americans might further the interests of the Indian nation-state. It mobilized the Indian community in 1987, with apparent success, to persuade Congress to withdraw the sale of sophisticated AWACS planes to Pakistan. The NFIA, NAAAID (National Association of American Asians of Indian Descent), and other organizations also gave their assistance on numerous occasions to the Indian government to help defeat legislation and resolutions, perceived to be inimical to India's welfare and interests, sponsored by Congressmen considered hostile to India—such as the relentless Republican Dan Burton (Indiana), co-founder and co-Chair of the Pakistan Caucus.

The Religious Life of
Indian Communities

Indians only numbered in the few thousands prior to the extensive overhaul of immigration regulations in 1965. It would, nonetheless, be a mistake to suppose that they left absolutely no impression upon American life or that as a microscopic minority they sought only to assimilate seamlessly into the dominant culture. Several examples of their contribution to American life, even before the reforms of 1965, readily come to mind. I have adverted to the Indian intellectuals who created something of a niche for themselves by their staunch advocacy of Gandhian non-violence, and to others who would be among the first generation of Indians to find academic positions at American universities. They are now largely forgotten figures, but in their own day they represented the public face of India to reasonably educated people in the United States.

One of the most prominent examples of the insertion of India into the American imagination comes, of course, from the life of Vivekananda. The leading disciple of the extraordinary nineteenth-century Bengali mystic, Sri Ramakrishna, Vivekananda was Hinduism's first and, some would say, to this day the most eminent representative of that faith to have arrived on American shores. It is doubtless a cliché, but one that inescapably confronts any student of Indian religions in the United States, to invoke Swami Vivekananda's electrifying address at the World Parliament of Religions in 1893 and the subsequent appeal that Vedanta came to have for a small but significant portion of the American elite. He had commenced his speech with five words, "Brothers and Sisters of America," that would leave an indelible imprint on everyone who heard them. Vivekananda traveled around the United States for two years, and in one city after another he received a rousing welcome. Mrs. John Henry Wright, who met him in August 1893, described him to her mother "as a most gorgeous vision. He had a superb carriage of the head, was very handsome in an oriental way, about thirty years old in time, ages in civilization." We repeatedly encounter descriptions of Vivekananda groaning under the accumulated weight of the stereotypes that were already well in place: unchanging India, the Oriental as timeless, the mystique of the East. Only six months later, Vivekananda would stop in Detroit on his whirlwind tour. "If Vive Kananda, the Brahmin monk," commented the *Detroit Journal*, "who is delivering a lecture tour in this city could be induced to remain for a week longer the largest hall in Detroit would not hold the crowds which would be anxious to hear him. He has become a veritable fad. . ." One newspaper chimed in with the remark that whenever Vivekananda was about to speak, "ladies, ladies everywhere filled the great auditorium."

The little town of Ganges in Michigan, which now houses the Vivekananda Monastery and Retreat, was established by an early follower of the Indian monk—as was, allegedly, the town of Nirvana, which is still standing. Many have at least passed through this Nirvana, even if the other nirvana is all but unattainable except to a handful of the truly enlightened. Swami Vivekananda established the Vedanta Society of New York in 1894, and another branch in San Francisco in 1900 on his second visit to the United States; and the institutionalization of Vedanta in America was well on its way. By 1929, there were Vedanta Centers in a number of other cities: Pittsburgh,

Boston, Providence, Portland, Chicago, and three in the Los Angeles area alone—Pasadena, Hollywood, and La Crescenta. The most interesting chapter of this history would be written in Southern California, where the young monk, Swami Prabhavananda, who had been sent to Hollywood by the Ramakrishna Order in 1929, eventually gathered a renowned group of British writers and intellectuals around him, including Aldous Huxley, Christopher Isherwood, and Gerald Heard, whose monastery at Trabuco Canyon was eventually gifted to the Vedanta Society. Prabhavananda and Isherwood together produced translations of a number of key Hindu philosophical texts—the *Bhagavad Gita*, Shankara's *Vivekachudamani*, and the Yoga Aphorisms of Patanjali—published in the Mentor Library series and so played a critical role in popularizing Indian philosophy. We might say that Hollywood's interest in "Eastern spirituality" was kindled by Isherwood, whose connections with film, art, and literary circles were prolific.

First there had been the "Hindu Invasion," *hordes* of Sikhs and a *tide* of turbans; and now the new phenomenon was captured by the title of Wendell Thomas's 1930 book, *Hinduism Invades America*. The author was at pains to explain that his work was not to be conceived "as an attack on Hinduism," nor meant to inflame popular American opinion "by pointing to a foreign menace;" rather, he thought of it as "a study of the amazing adventure of an Eastern faith in a Western land." Thomas documented what appeared to him to be an explosion of interest in Hinduism in America, and he thought it plausible that "Hinduism, with its conception of vital evolutionary progress toward a divine goal, will be just the religion we need to keep us from atheism in a scientific age." Not only had learned Hindu lecturers visited America, but, the Ramakrishna movement aside, many popularizers of Hinduism had made their way to America and there were even "American imposters passing for Hindu popular lecturers."

Thomas was most struck by the Yagoda Satsang Society of America, founded by Yogananda in 1925 and later transformed into the Self-Realization Fellowship. Yogananda had arrived in the U.S. in 1920, and soon came to the realization that American audiences would be most receptive to his teachings if he could establish not merely that religion and science were compatible but that India's yogic traditions constituted a science of religion. He emphasized that religion did not reside only in texts, however venerable they might be, but rather that India's yogic traditions aimed to move the spiritual candidate to ever increasing levels of spiritual awareness and self-realization, much like the scientist who seeks to perfect an experiment in the laboratory. Though Thomas wrote long before the heyday of the Self-Realization Fellowship, which by the mid-1930s had come to stand in for Hinduism in the U.S., he was shrewd enough to realize that Yogananda had a "genius for organization," was sensitive to the fact that his teachings should be easily reconciled with "modern business methods and financial ambition for success," and understood that it was necessary to master American methods of commerce and advertising to turn his teachings on yoga and self-realization into a marketable product.

Only Yogananda could give a talk, such as one before the Rotary Club at Buffalo, on "How to Recharge Your Business Battery Out of the Cosmos." American holidays were celebrated at the Self-Realization Fellowship's headquarters in Los Angeles with great fanfare, and Thomas described how Yogananda had garnered national attention by prescribing "a meatless diet" for President Coolidge "to keep him cool!" The Vedanta swamis, Thomas wrote, "are still Hindus, while Swami Yogananda, as it were, is a naturalized American." As Thomas put it brilliantly, "It is clear that Swami Yogananda is even more American in method than in message." Yogananda published *Autobiography of a Yogi* in 1946: it became a runaway bestseller, and has ever since remained in print. Those who marvel at the success of the modern-day Indian American master of spiritual capitalism, Deepak Chopra, who has merely refined Yogananda's methods, characteristically in the most American idiom by simplifying teachings to "seven steps," ten rules, and the like, should look back to Yogananda to understand the lineage in which Chopra was able to place himself so effortlessly.

Whatever the presence of Vedanta, yoga, and other "Hindu" teachings in American life from the 1920s until the 1960s, it is necessary to remind ourselves that such teachings were being consumed overwhelmingly by Americans and that the Census of 1960 was able to account for a paltry 8,745 Indians in the entire country. The religious, cultural, and social life of diasporic Indian groups only took on a new vibrancy in the post-1965 period, most particularly after the community had found its feet. Hazrat Inayat Khan, a renowned Sufi teacher from India, made his way to the United States in 1912, and three years later the Sikhs, who comprised the bulk of the Indian immigrant community at that juncture in history, established a gurdwara in Stockton, California. This gurdwara attracted Hindus as well, and long served as the focal point of the religious lives of most Indians. But by far the greater majority of Indians who have arrived in the U.S. since 1965 are Hindus, and it is not surprising that Hinduism's growth has perhaps been the most spectacular. Swami A.C. Bhaktivedanta, a Bengali Vaishnava who claimed to be in the direct spiritual lineage of the great bhakta Chaitanya Mahaprabhu, arrived in the U.S. in 1965 and established the International Society of Krishna Consciousness [ISKCON]. He acquired a very considerable following, and the Hare Krsnas, as his followers were dubbed, were soon a ubiquitous presence at airports and university campuses. They chanted at street corners, passed out Hindu religious literature and their monthly magazine, *Back to Godhead*, and enticed the general public with generous offerings of food. For many years, for instance, they have taken out annual processions with chariots on the occasion of Janmashtami, the birthday of Krishna, and the "Chariot Festival" in Los Angeles concludes at Venice Beach where a free modest vegetarian meal is dished out to thousands of people amidst grand festivities. Any systematic history of vegetarianism in the United States would have to take account of the part played by the Hare Krsnas in popularizing vegetarianism, and it is much more probable, though this point demands sustained sociological inquiry, that Indian restaurants, including those managed by the Hare Krsnas, remain the mainstay of the slowly growing numbers of Americans who are attracted to vegetarianism.

In the incipient years of the Hare Krsna movement, when temples built by immigrant Hindus were few and far between, Indians frequented the ISKCON temples though few Hindus joined the movement. Sometimes the Hare Krsna temple was the only Hindu edifice in town and even came to serve as a small community center. By the mid-1970s, the Indian population had registered considerable growth and put down roots, and the community could think of commissioning new temples or converting existing unused structures, such as churches, into temples and community centers. Comprised largely of professionals, who had little experience in, or inclination towards, philanthropic activities, the Indian community began to direct much of its affluence towards the construction of new temples. The growth of temples in the Chicago area, particularly in the 1980s, illustrates amply the history of Hinduism in the United States. The 1980 census recorded 33,541 Indians in the Chicago metropolitan region; in 1990, the number had grown to 56,462, and to 125,208 by 2000. Indians have now surpassed Filipinos as the largest ethnic Asian community in the Chicago area. In December 1977, the Hindu Temple of Greater Chicago (HTGC) had been founded as a not-for-profit organization. Over the next few years, its members, many of whom were wealthy doctors and other professionals, raised funds for the construction of a temple and in 1981 they purchased a seventeen-acre site for $300,000 in Lemont. The HTGC website states that "the complex has two separate temples. They provide a congenial atmosphere for worship, spiritual advancement and also serve as a focal point for cultural and educational activities." The two temples in question are a Ganesh temple, which was inaugurated by the immensely popular singer Lata Mangeshkar in 1985, and was subsequently expanded to house the deities of Shiva and Durga, and a larger Rama temple for which the *kumbhabisekham* or formal dedication was held on July 4, 1986. The Rama temple "is built to specifications in the authentic style of the Chola dynasty," while the Ganesh-Shiva-Durga [GSD] Temple emulates the architecture of Bhuvaneshwar, Orissa. The Shiva-Vishnu temple in Livermore, California displays an identical form of architectural eclecticism.

The HTGC temple complex, however, was to be many years in the making, and by the early 1980s the Telugu professionals in the Greater Chicago area had committed themselves to a construction of a Sri Venkateswara or Balaji Temple in Aurora, also in the western suburbs. The groundbreaking ceremony in 1985 was attended by former Indian Prime Minister Morarji Desai, and Muttaialstapathy, who is an expert on temple construction in south India, and the Chicago-based architect Subhas Nadkarni, who have since worked together on the recently opened Hindu Temple of Central Florida (Orlando), were brought together to collaborate on the design of the temple. A handsome structure, which has to date cost more than $4 million, the Balaji temple, housed on a sprawling seventy-one-acre site, has shrines to Lakshmi, Andal, Ganapati, Subrahmanyam, Shiva, and Parvati. Its opulence is, nonetheless, exceeded by the magnificent Shri Swaminarayan Mandir, which opened in Bartlett, some forty miles from Chicago, in August 2004. This temple, which cost over $30 million, uses limestone from Turkey and marble from Italy and Makrana (India), and nearly 500 craftsmen in India labored over the 108 marble pillars which support fifteen domes. One might argue that the Bochasanwasi Shri Akshar Purushottam Swaminarayan (BAPS) Sanstha, one of the three groups of the Swaminarayan sect to whom the temple belongs, is prone to ostentatious temple architecture, and the Bartlett temple follows on the heels of monumental BAPS temples at Akshardham (outside Ahmedabad, Gujarat) and Neasden (in north London) which have become major tourist attractions. But the indisputable fact remains that as the Indian community acquires increasing influence, and gains self-confidence, it has sought to mark its presence by grand religious edifices. The Chicago region is now served by nearly twenty temples, as well as three gurdwaras, several mosques, at least one major Jain temple, and even a church affiliated with the Malankara Orthodox Syrian Church of India. In the distant suburbs, the Indian Muslim community is served by a mosque in Schaumberg and a gleaming new gurdwara in Palatine caters to Sikhs.

It is possible to speak at this juncture of "Temple Hinduism" and of certain marked characteristics taken on by the faith in its new setting. Where before temples were, on the whole, casual affairs, and immigrants showed a willingness to adapt to diasporic conditions, now many temples are increasingly ostentatious affairs. It is not merely, as I have already suggested, that million-dollar temples are becoming, if one may exaggerate, as common as million-dollar homes. A certain turn towards textualism appears to have become more pronounced with the growing affluence of the community. Temples are increasingly built to conform to the specifications encountered in the *shilpa sastras*, or manuals of temple architecture. Specialists versed in temple architecture are likely to be hired as consultants. The temples are decidedly grander, but communities seem much less disposed to innovate or negotiate with other communities. A proposed BAPS temple in Chino Hills, an affluent portion of San Bernadino County in southern California, was the subject of much dispute in the city council meeting in 2004, where it was demanded that the proposed temple spires, from fifty-two to eighty feet, be reduced so that they did not exceed the forty-three-foot height limit stipulated in the city code. However, BAPS representatives refused to entertain the suggestion, putting forward the argument that the proportions specified in the *sastras* could not be violated. BAPS representatives could nonetheless have preserved the inviolability of the proportions by lowering not only the temple spires but also altering all other dimensions of the temple and its images by the same ratio.

Secondly, not only are the images carved in India, as one would expect, but priests continue to be drawn to this day from India. There are notable exceptions: the priests at the Shri Lakshmi Narayan Mandir in Richmond Hill, New York, which services largely Indo-Guyanese now settled on the East Coast, are themselves drawn from this community. As some members of the community moved to Orlando, where a branch of the temple was opened in 1992, the priests followed in their wake. The

Indo-Guyanese diaspora already has such a complex history of its own that one is not surprised that members of this community feel more comfortable with priests who share their history. Wherever in India or in the wider Indian diaspora Hindu priests may have been drawn from, they often go American—embracing cell phones, credit cards, even American slang. But, from the standpoint of worshippers, the priests still bear marks of a cultural and religious authenticity. The history of the Shri Lakshmi Narayan temple is illustrative of a third marked tendency, namely the fact that many temples are associated with distinct Hindu communities. The clientele at the various Sri Venkatesvara temples is largely of South Indian origins, just as the Swaminarayan temples are patronized overwhelmingly by Gujaratis. Murugan temples, likewise, attract mainly Tamilians. Unarguably, there is nothing exceptional in this at all, but what we might call a regional sectarianism persists even when communities are quite small—and even when, as we shall see, simultaneous claims about how the United States furnishes hope for a less divisive Hinduism are implicitly advanced to project the notion of Indian American Hindus as constituting something of a vanguard for the faith.

It is possible, at the same time, to speak of three distinct if related forms in which Hinduism's history in the United States is most productively written in the idiom of pluralism. A large metropolitan center such as Los Angeles is home to a Murugan temple, at least two Radha Krishna temples, a Kali Mandir, a Devi Mandir, a Sanatan Dharma Mandir, a Lakshmi Narayan Mandir, a Sri Venkateswara temple, and close to a dozen other temples. The nondescript Valley Hindu Temple of Northridge, where a sizable Indian community has developed over the last two decades, is representative of the other, nonsectarian tradition of Hindu temples in the United States, insofar as the temple houses a diverse array of deities—Shiva, Ram, Krishna, Durga, Lakshmi, to name a few—and welcomes Hindus of all persuasions. It has sometimes been suggested that Hindus in the diaspora may be less attentive to distinctions which hold sway in India, such as those between north and south, Vaishnavites and Saivites, and so on. Whether this is partly on account of their own minority status in the U.S. is an interesting and yet unresolved question. Whether this phenomenon is as distinct as is sometimes argued is also somewhat questionable. While images of both Vishnu and Shiva are not usually housed under one roof in Hindu temples in India, and the mythological works known as the Puranas—where the history, genealogy, and worship of these gods is articulated—are exceedingly sectarian, the Puranas are less exclusive than is commonly argued. Thus, a Vaishnava Purana usually elevates Vishnu as the supreme God but still has ample room for Shiva; a Saivite Purana inverses the order. A Devi Purana, dedicated to the Goddess, will similarly render secondary the male gods.

We might describe the Vishnu-Shiva-Devi complex as the agonistic structure of popular Hinduism. But perhaps it is also an aspect of the playfulness of the gods. At the brand new Hindu Temple of Central Florida (Orlando), where a substantial portion of the pan-Indian Hindu pantheon is to be found, one gopuram (gate) is described as being in the Chola style, the other in the "Naga" or northern Indian style. The temple's board of trustees claims that Hinduism is synonymous with diversity, and that Hindu temples in the U.S. must attempt to meet the varying requirements of Hindu communities and their styles of worship. But this clichéd claim about diversity, which has now reached the point of monotonous excess in American culture, is much more substantive than it appears, since the supposition is that the practice of Hinduism in the United States more likely approximates the ideal of Hinduism than Hinduism as it is encountered in India.

Secondly, though commentators have occasionally commented on the social aloofness of Indians, and Indian shopkeepers have sometimes been criticized for keeping their stores open on July 4th, which is celebrated with fanfare as Independence Day, Hindu and Sikh communities are more cognizant of American mores and customs, indeed even the country's physical geography, than is commonly recognized. The Rama shrine at the Hindu Temple of Greater Chicago was consecrated on July 4th, and we can be certain that the temple's trustees and devotees held to the view that Hindus not only share in the (purported) blessings of American "freedom," but that Hinduism enables a more enriched and spiritual conception of freedom with its stress on spiritual emancipation and self-realization. As Indian American Hindus would be inclined to argue, July the Fourth marks not only the emergence of an American nation stitched together from diverse strands, all encapsulated in the formula, *E Pluribus Unum*, "From Many, One," but also, keeping in mind the principles of the Declaration of Independence, the public and secular affirmation of the timeless wisdom of the Hindus, captured most succinctly in the Vedic notion, "Truth is One; Sages Name It Variously" (*Rig Veda* 1.164.46). Arriving on the shores of the New World, Columbus thought that he had wound up in India; but with the firm landing of Indians on American soil, that mistake has finally been rectified. Hindus, on this vision, help America to be a fulfilled place, lending poignancy all of their own to the meaning of July 4th. By the same token, Hindus feel immensely grateful to America: July the Fourth, having taken an ancient truth and democratized it, has now brought Vedic teachings into the global public sphere.

One scholar has written of the famous Sri Venkateswara Temple in Penn Hills, Pennsylvania, on which construction started in 1976, the bicentennial of the American Revolution, that while it does not ignore the Hindu festival calendar, "it tries as far as is astrologically possible to plan big events around the holidays of the American secular calendar." Yet even more remarkable than these attempts at temporal commensurability is the Hinduization of American landscapes. The Penn Hills temple stands at the intersection, according to a souvenir published by temple authorities, at the confluence of the Allegheny, Monongahela, and "the subterranean river," an unmistakable allusion to Prayag in north-central India, where the Yamuna, Ganga, and the underground Saraswati rivers by popular belief converge and thus lend the place its extraordinary sanctity. Not any less remarkable is the temple complex of Barsana Dham, a 200-acre property in the neighborhood of Austin, Texas, which emulates Barsana where Radha, ordinarily represented as the consort and favorite companion of Krishna, is herself worshipped as indivisibly one with Krishna. Established in 1990,

Barsana Dham was designed as a representation of the holy land of Braj in north India where Krishna and Radha frolicked on the green and performed the celestial dance (raslila). In the naturally more pious tone of the web site [www.barsanadham. org], "all the important holy places of Braj like Govardhan, Radha Kund, Prem Sarovar, Shyam Kuti and Mor Kuti are represented in Barsana Dham where the natural stream, named Kalinidi, represents the Yamuna river of Vrindavan."

Finally, while religion never occupies the space merely marked as "religion," Hinduism, Sikhism, and Jainism in the United States have begun to radiate outwards to embrace a much wider array of sociocultural life forms. The actual space of the temple complex allows an array of activities that in India were traditionally not tolerated under a single roof, though the practices of temple worship in India are similarly undergoing some change in a few places. In neighborhood temples in Delhi, for instance, I have sometimes seen homeopathic doctors setting up clinics. Among the definitions of Hinduism widely prevalent in Hindu communities, none is perhaps as frequently encountered as the claim that "Hinduism is a way of life rather than a religion." The cultural centers associated with many temples seem designed to vindicate that worldview. Thus the Hindu temple, with or without a formally designated "cultural center" alongside, might very well offer bharatnatyam classes, instruction in yoga and Indian languages (especially Hindi), and lessons in Indian instrumental music (particularly the sitar and tabla). The concept of "Sunday school" has its enthusiasts among Hindus, and children are enjoined to learn "Hindu values" or "the dharmic approach to life," familiarize themselves with religious texts, and embrace the rich culture and heritage of India. Hindu temple societies typically conduct a "Bal Vihar" on Sundays, and often the cultural centers offer senior citizens a public forum for conviviality. Hindu temples and cultural centers often mobilize resources when natural disasters—in the last decade, most prominently the Orissa Cyclone, the Gujarat Earthquake, and the Indian Ocean Tsunami—have struck India.

Indian "Culture" in the Diaspora

There are multiple spaces, of course, in which what is taken to be Indian culture not only thrives but is reified, just as a new generation of Indian Americans have embraced literature, art, and music to combat racism, gender discrimination, and neo-imperialism, forge solidarities with other—generally less priv-ileged—minorities, and give expression to their conception of politics, public life, and social activism. Indian Americans, like most people, are accustomed to a traditional conception of political life, where politics is construed to mean enrollment in one of the two (largely indistinguishable, one might add) po-litical parties, running for public office, and taking an interest in America's relations with India and Pakistan. But some in the community are now beginning to recognize that political participation can take many forms, and that there is something that might be called cultural activism. While Urvashi Vaid, an Indian American who served as the media director, and then the executive director, of the National Gay and Lesbian Task Force (NGLTF) is far from being a household name in middle-class Indian American families, who eagerly watch for signs showing that Indian participation in the electoral process is increasing, it is clear that the conception of the political among some Indian communities has shifted and is fundamentally informed by identity politics, multiculturalism, the pressing question of lifestyle choices, and a concern about the geopolitics of culture.

Similarly, while the "coming out" stories of gays and lesbians may not interest everyone, and many will view such stories as intensely personal narratives about sexual freedom, the participation of Trikone, a gay South Asian group, in the annual San Francisco Gay Pride Parade was viewed by its members as a demonstration of the maturation of South Asian political culture. The apparently seamless shift in my own description of gay culture from "Indian" to "South Asian" reflects not an ignorance about the complex politics of being "Indian" in the United States, but rather an awareness of the historical contingencies under which culture operates as a sign of the political. Many South Asian lesbians and gays have written about how South Asians are not quite viewed as "Asians" even in queer groups and organizations; on the other hand, when Indian, Pakistani, and other Asian gays and lesbians sought to march at the India Day Parade in New York in 1994 as members of the South Asian Lesbian and Gay Association (SALGA), the Federation of Indian Associations (FIA) denied them a permit, ostensibly on the grounds the parade was only open to Indian, not South Asian, groups. One suspects, of course, that the FIA, which is no paragon of liberal values, was inclined to view Indian homosexuals as an embarrassment to the Indian community, indeed as not quite "Indian."

Whatever the negotiations, howsoever imperceptible, that always take place whenever culture is evoked, there is a tendency among many Indian Americans to reify Indian culture as something that is almost eternal, rooted to timeless traditions, imbibed with mother's breast milk, a comfort zone of certainties, a repository of known moral values—in short, something that is a rather good thing. One is as likely to hear this at Hindu temples as at events, such as a Bharatnatyam recital, organized by the community. The complaint most frequently encountered among Indian teenagers and even college students is that their parents have forbidden them to date before marriage, and an ar-

gument is put before adolescents and youngsters that such behavior is not countenanced by "Indian culture." Many Indian
American students who were often taken to India during their
childhood and have some familiarity with the country remark
that their parents' notion of Indian culture has little correspondence to the culture of youth at colleges and universities in large
metropolitan centers in India if not in smaller cities and towns.
Many Indian students in the United States keep their premari-
tal sexual relationships an absolute secret from their parents,
and the taboo on any mention of inter-racial relationships is, if
anything, even more strictly observed. But, to take another example, those who are inclined to the study of literature, history,
or the performing arts, rather than engineering, medicine, or
business administration, are similarly apprehensive about dis-
cussing their plans with their parents, though here few would
be prepared to advance the claim that Indian culture rather
than practical considerations are likely to make Indian parents
fume at their children's choices. If my own experience as an
educator is any guide, every Indian American professor in my
position has also served as a counselor and therapist to students
who, when inclined to pursue graduate work in the humanities or the softer social sciences, are terrified of making known
their preferences to their parents who have long imagined that
their sons and daughters would be successful engineers or lawyers. The obvious desire among parents to see their children
succeed in some profession that brings both pecuniary success
and status to its practitioners notwithstanding, one cannot but
still wonder whether "culture" is implicated in the stereotypical
representation of Indians as doctors, engineers, and computer
professionals.

It is widely recognized that Indians dominate the National
Spelling Bee, having produced the national champion in five
of the last nine years, but is there anything specifically to be
found in "Indian culture" that is conducive to such success?
Indian parents of winners and other contestants attribute the
success of their children to hard work, discipline, high moti-
vation, the premium placed on educational attainments, and
even on the desire of recent immigrant communities to partake

in the American dream and show that they have arrived. But much of this is also true of Korean-Americans, Chinese-Americans, and some other ethnic groups, and the question remains how Indians came to acquire something of a dominance over the Spelling Bee. Here is one instance among many of how a minority may subscribe to the notion of itself as a "model minority." A somewhat more sociological explanation would perhaps stress the fact that Indian students to a disproportionately high degree come from highly educated families and that knowledge of English, which is almost a native tongue to many Indians in the United States, confers advantages on Indians denied to other ethnic groups. Yet the evidence from the Census Bureau's latest reports on this question is somewhat ambiguous. The Asian Community Survey of February 2007, based on data collected in 2004, shows that Japanese and even Filipinos far outstrip Indian Americans in describing English as the language that is spoken at home; however, among people who claimed that English was not spoken at their home, or was not at any rate the predominant language of everyday conversation, Indians easily outnumbered all other Asians in describing themselves as speaking English "very well." One might also take the view that all immigrant communities attempt to create particular niches for themselves, and that Indians excel in spelling bees just as Dominicans dominate American baseball and Kenyans and Ethiopians appear to have monopolized long-distance running.

The difference here is that baseball has a huge following in the Dominican Republic, just as the longer races, extending from 5,000 meters to the marathon, have been part of the repertoire of Kenyans and Ethiopians in their own country for some time; however, by contrast, the "Spelling Bee" is a cultural artifact of American society that has no resonance in India itself. It may well be the case that the present generation of affluent middle-class Indians settled in Bangalore and Mumbai who are plotting futures in the United States may already be preparing their very young children in India for the near future when the family will be comfortably settled in an American suburb and the children will be memorizing the spelling of arcane words, but there is no evidence yet that the institution of the Spelling Bee has winged its way to India. (British rather than American spellings prevail in India, though with Britain's diminishing influence in Indian life this legacy of the Raj may soon show signs of fracture—and perhaps the American institution of the spelling bee will add its own color to the demise of the world of colour.) When a particular community is viewed as having a stranglehold over some profession, trade, or cultural phenomenon, other communities might be inclined to direct their resources elsewhere. Thus success breeds more success. It can well be argued, however, that all these interpretations fall quite short in their explanatory power, and that many Indians themselves might not have an adequate understanding of the manner in which they are able to call upon certain cultural resources. Indian intellectual traditions persist in continuing to emphasize memorization, and various mnemonic devices are still deployed in various Indian traditions for the retention of texts. Thus "Indian culture" may well be a potent factor in understanding why Indian Americans have nearly monopolized the spelling bee, though this is not the Indian culture that students and their parents have in mind when they are probed by outsiders. The gripping film *Spellbound*, not to be confused with Hitchcock's film of the same name, amply demonstrates that the narrative Indian American parents wish to hold on to is one which emphasizes hard work, discipline, perseverance, success, and pride of integration into American society.

In private conversation, many Indians, particularly of the first generation, have been known to suggest that America is sadly wanting in "culture," and that American youth culture, in particular, can only have a detrimental effect on the lives of the young. Culture, so conceived, has little relation to high art, literature, or music. There might not have been many Indian Americans, especially from the 1960s to the 1980s, who took much of an interest in American literature, much less in the rarified world of Western classical music and opera. The numbers who frequented amusement parks, such as Disneyland and Great America, would have been much larger, but they would not have recognized such excursions as expressions of genuine cultural activity either. The visit to the theme park, which was held up as a model of how much more technologically advanced America was than India, was a more elaborate, fun-packed version of the picnic outing to which the Indian middle-class person was accustomed from his or her time in India. In thinking of "culture," the Indian American immigrant was much more inclined to think of everyday practices, norms, and protocols of behavior. Thus, when the Indian American was heard complaining of the lack of culture in American society, it encompassed not only, as one might predict, the grievance that youngsters did not pay enough deference to the old, but also, to take a few examples, the complaints that Americans paid little attention to manners, were somewhat negligent in their attentiveness to the needs of children, and were grossly deficient in traditions of hospitality. Behind all this, some Indian Americans never allowed themselves to forget that though they came to the United States as, so to speak, supplicants for better economic standards and a life of new opportunities, they were the representatives of an ancient civilization at the doors of a new country which had much to learn in the way of culture.

Indian culture, in this scenario, is also visualized as something of an anodyne that ameliorates American culture's corrosive influence on the young. The activities of the Indian Student Union (ISU), which is to be found at virtually every college and university where a sizable body of Indian students exist, provide a good illustration of what is taken to be wholesome Indian culture. At many institutions, even though the ISU is a standing organization, receiving funding as a student body, it remains relatively inactive except for an annual culture show. At two elite universities with which I have considerable familiarity, the University of California, Los Angeles (UCLA), which has some 800 second-generation Indian American undergraduates and several hundred graduate students of Indian origin, and the University of Chicago, with an Indian undergraduate student body of around 350, the culture show dominates the ISU's yearly agenda. Each year's show is supposed to revolve around a theme, often designated by a term of Sanskrit origin.

At UCLA, the Indian Student Union in 2002 presented a show described as "*Samjhotha*: Understanding Our Experience." The word "samjhota" in fact means agreement, or compromise between parties involved in a dispute. The following year, the ISU presented "Astitva," and in later years the annual shows have been described as offerings of "Sambhavana: Our Choices, Our Lives" (2005), though the word is best translated as likelihood or possibility, and as "*Dhrishya*: Where Futures Align" (2006). It is doubtful that even the Hindi-speaking students in the second-generation have any real familiarity with these words; more likely than not, the students took their cue from Hindi films. The printed program is invariably funded with full-page advertisements by the Princeton Review and Kaplan, two standardized test coaching centers that help students prepare for admissions tests for law, business, medical, and graduate schools.

The most pertinent fact is that the shows have no relation to the announced theme. Had the shows been encompassed under the rubric of such terms as "sanskriti" (culture), "sadhana" (discipline), or "anubhava" (experience), it would have made no difference to the content. Year after year, the pattern is pretty much the same and loosely follows a tripartite structure. There is a large component on the folk and classical dances of India, and Bharatnatyam and Kathak are complemented by a fisherman's folk dance from Kerala, the Gujarati Garba, a Rajasthani dance, the Punjabi Bhangra, perhaps an instrumental piece, and so on. One can think of this exercise as a miniature version of the annual Republic Day parade in New Delhi, showcasing the diversity and variegated culture of India. There is no awareness among the Indian American students that their peers in India long ceased to have any interest in folk culture, except when it might be marshaled as evidence in some political argument, and that "folk dances" are now strictly consumption items for Hindi film sets, foreign tourists, non-resident Indians (NRIs), and others in quest of some authentic India. Secondly, there are Bollywood numbers, a mélange of old and new songs, the new ones generally in remix, as well as one specimen each of hip hop and "fusion." Though the young themselves have little interest in older songs, they have heard them at home and recognize that their parents view such songs as what in Indian English is called "evergreen."

The dance and music numbers are interspersed by one long skit, or several short ones; but, with utter predictability, the subject of the humorous skits is the identity of Indian Americans, and the conflict between the first and second generations over dating, marriage, and lifestyle choices. Middle-aged bespectacled Indian ladies, or "aunties" as they are known, are shown, according to a set formula, as anxiety-ridden over the future of their children and the difficulty of finding good matches in the diasporic setting. Comic relief comes in the form of a gentle imitation of an immigrant fresh off the boat (FOB), or a narration of the travails of an innocent Indian caught in the whirlwind of globalization. The entire purpose of the exercise, quoting from the brochure marking the 2006 show, "Dhrishya," is to leave the student with the assurance that "at the end of the day, even if he or she is a global citizen, an Indian is an Indian, whether in Dubai, Mumbai, or UCLA." The Indian parents leave with the satisfaction that their children, though away from home, have not entirely drifted away from Indian culture and cut loose into the "junglee" or wild culture of American society. Politics, even in the narrowest conception of the term, is never allowed to intrude into this world of healthy, insulated Indian culture. Thus, though hate crimes against South Asians, particularly Sikhs (whose turbans were taken by some to mean that they were Muslims, even followers of Osama bin Laden), rose dramatically after September 11, 2001, the 2002 and 2003 culture shows at UCLA offered not the slightest hint of this violence or of the aggressively anti-immigrant sentiments that were openly on display in the wider American society.

Not only is Indian culture perhaps more stable in the U.S. than it is in India, but it also pivots around fewer phenomena that are supposedly emblematic of Indian and especially Hindu culture. An astounding number of daughters from middle-class and professional Indian American families are tutored in Indian dance, predominantly in bharatnatyam. Though many commentators, myself included, have rendered bharatnatyam as "the dance of India [Bharat]," the term is more accurately drawn from the dance (*natya*) form around which a manual was written by the ancient writer Bharata. The diasporic history of Bharatnatyam, often postulated as a reinvented tradition in recent feminist scholarship, illustrates well how the reification of Indian traditions has been shaped through the vehicle of Indian womanhood. Indian women are understood to be not only the keepers of the hearth, but the custodians and carriers of culture: they are the sign of all that is permanent, enduring and mythic in a culture, just as the man is the sign of the modern and the transient. Indian men may give up their pajamas and dhotis as they take to the boardrooms of corporations and stock exchanges, but the Indian woman, to evoke the common sentiment, is never lovelier than when a sari is draped around her lissome figure.

In the form of Bharatnatyam, the Indian woman is the dance, energy, and elegance of India, the embodiment of the timeless culture (*sanskriti*) of an ancient civilization—and in the diaspora, where anxieties about cultural loss and contamination are pervasive, and the resources for the renewal of a spiritual outlook are comparatively fewer, Bharatnatyam has had to take on the onerous burden of providing a spiritual and cultural anchor for young women. Correspondingly, some bharatnatyam teachers in the U.S. have become institutions unto themselves, commanding fees and audiences comparable to what only the best teachers in India attain, as well as the unswerving adulation of their pupils. The Chicago-based dance company, Natyakalalayam, founded by Hema Rajagopalan in the mid-1970s, undertook 121 performances in the U.S. in 1999 alone, including some at major venues such as the Kennedy Center in Washington, D.C. Another famous teacher in Los Angeles, who also has a faculty position at a major university, reportedly has 250 students. Initiation under her has also come to mean that the student must eventually subscribe to what we might call the "arangetram package." This teacher requires, moreover, each student to attend the *arangetram*, or first public recital, of all other students in the same cohort. The family of the pupil puts on a lavish show and reception, with costs commonly running to as much as $30,000. Though these families may not be paying dowries for their daughters, they are now running up "arangetram debts."

Such is the view of bharatnatyam as the supreme symbol of refined Indian culture that even a few Pakistani and Bangladeshi Muslim families, oblivious of vicious gossip and innuendo among more orthodox Muslims, have been known to expose their daughters to its charms. This is all the more remarkable, and indeed admirable, in view of Bharatnatyam's South Indian origins in the institution of temple dancers (*devadasis*) acting under royal patronage, a tradition that colonial observers sought to render as one in which the *devadasis* were prostituted to their patrons. Bharatnatyam remains a staple at Indian student culture shows, Diwali melas (fairs), Indian Independence day festivities, and the state-sponsored "Festival of India." The other mainstay of all such cultural events is the Bhangra, which is as boisterous as Bharatnatyam is staid and elegant. Indeed, Bhangra, which has also become immensely popular in recent years, has become rapidly institutionalized in its own fashion. There are now nearly 200 independent and college teams, the greater majority of them founded less than five years ago, and they appear in some two dozen annual bhangra competitions across the United States with names such as "Bhangra Blast" (Boston), "Bhangra Blizzard" (Buffalo), "Bhangra Blowout" (Washington, DC), and "Bhangra Dhamaka [Thud]" (Durham). Some competition venues hold 3,000 to 4,000 seats, and bhangra has enough of a following that tickets are now available through a central vendor [bhangratickets.com]. Bhangra is a reminder to Indians, as much as a demonstration to all others, that a "model minority" and nerdy Silicon Valley types can also have fun. Moreover, the verdant green of the Punjab with its fields of mustard greens, the backdrop to bhangra, stands-in for the simple living that the immigrant Indian has had to forgo in the rat-race of (sub)urban American living. Bhangra both tames and fulfills the immigrant's instinct to return to the relatively less complicated life left behind in India; for the second generation Indian, who has no memories of the smell of the earth in Punjab, it is an expression of Indian culture in its most vivacious, authentic, manly incarnation.

A more aggressive, and consequently narrower, conception of Indian culture is championed by the Hindu Students Council (HSC), the youth division of the Vishwa Hindu Parishad (VHP, www.vhp.org), an organization founded in 1964 to promote Hindu culture worldwide. The VHP is more commonly thought of as the vanguard of Hindutva, as performing the cultural work of militant Hindu nationalism alongside the Rashtriya Swayamsevak Sangh (RSS), a paramilitary organization which has traditionally been represented as militant Hinduism's muscleman, and the Bharatiya Janata Party (BJP), which is a political party that governed India for several years at the head of a coalition and is now well-represented in the Indian Parliament as the principal opposition party. In fact, the VHP unabashedly champions a highly chauvinistic conception of Hinduism and of "Hindu Rashtra" or a Hindu nation-state, but at least overseas, where it has become increasingly active over the last decade, it prefers to work unobtrusively, maintaining almost a shadowy presence. The American branch of the VHP [www.vhp-america.org] commenced work in 1970 in New York and is now active throughout the U.S. The VHP has attracted a large body of scholarship, some of it directed to an interrogation of its fund-raising activities and recruitment drives in the United States, but much less work has been done on its main front—the Hindu Students Council (HSC, www.hscnet.org).

With about seventy-five chapters across the United States, the Hindu Students Council, which claims to be the largest Hindu student group outside India, has traveled a long distance from its beginnings at Northeastern University in 1987. Its birth and continued growth can be attributed to the convergence at educational institutions of second-generation Indian American students and graduate students from India. One consequence of the growing Indian population is the increased visibility of Indian American students on American college and university campuses. These "heritage students," as they are known to the faculty, have sometimes been vocal in their demand for courses on Indian history, religion, and culture, and oftentimes a more enhanced course offering focused on Hinduism is their most immediate concern. In the spring quarter of the 2001–2002 academic year, to take one example, the Stanford Hindu Students Council successfully persuaded a professor from the university's Religious Studies Department to co-sponsor alongside the HSC a course entitled "Hinduism in the Modern Era." It is understandable that Hinduism's onward march in the twentieth century, and Modern Hindu Spiritual Movements, should have been on the agenda, but a week devoted to the subject of "Hindus as Minorities" suggests how far some of Stanford's Hindu students have succumbed to the claims embodied in Hindu nationalist writings about Hinduism's endangered history in the present world. Over the last decade, many of the "heritage" students have moved into the HSC, which was at its inception generally led by single male students from India pursuing higher degrees in engineering, computer sciences, and the natural sciences, and increasingly leadership is now being exercised by second-generation Indian Americans.

The Hindu Student Council's other stated aim is to bolster the faith of Hindu students on campus, giving Hindu students the same opportunities of worship and fellowship which Christian, Jewish, and Muslim students have claimed for themselves through their religious groups. They have also frequently sponsored campus visits by advocates of militant Hinduism, such as David Frawley and Koenrad Elst; they take special pride in, among other Indians, the likes of the ayurveda guru Deepak Chopra, who is seen as a supreme instance of the most judicious East-West blend, a fount of Hindu wisdom who has mastered Western techniques of marketing. Chopra is celebrated as the kind of Indian who, having stayed close to the spiritual roots of a timeless Hindu civilization, has not only shown that the material inheritance of Western civilization—its energy, spirit of technological innovation, and appreciation of the blessings of the free market—can be inherited by people all over the world, but who has utilized his knowledge of the West to market aggressively the virtues of Hindu civilization before the world. There is little understanding of the fact that Chopra, who is perhaps savvier than they realize, seldom if ever uses the word "Hindu" to promote ayurveda or self-awareness, relying instead on such anodyne phrases as "ancient Indian spirituality" or "traditional Indian culture." The organizational strengths of the HSC can reasonably be surmised from the fact that in 1993, on the centenary of Vivekananda's address to the World Parliament of Religions, it held a "Vision 2000 Global Youth Conference" attended by 2,000 Hindu students from the U.S., India, and nearly twenty other foreign countries. Vivekananda is arguably the patron saint of the HSC, the figure from the relatively recent past who is most admired as someone who evokes the idea of a resurgent India achieving conquest over the world with its rich spiritual inheritance. It is Vivekananda who, from the standpoint of the Vishwa Hindu Parishad and the Hindu Students Council, successfully transformed Hinduism from an inward-looking faith to the global religion that it had once aspired to be as it spread through Thailand, Java, Bali, and Indochina. Thus the Hindu Student Council's "Global Dharma Conference," held at Edison, New Jersey, in 2003, is not only a tribute to Vivekananda's conception of Hinduism as a global religion but an affirmation of Hinduism's capacity to organize its devotees and take its place alongside other world religions.

The Politics of Affluence
and the Anxiety of Influence

The Indian American landscape has, in some crucial respects, vastly changed over the last two decades, and the Indian appropriation of the motel, which stands at the nexus of narratives that have become almost sacrosanct in American folklore, serves, as well as any other socioeconomic and cultural phenomenon, to illustrate the depth of the changes. On May 7, 1979, the *Washington Post* carried an article detailing the entrepreneurial acumen and network of Patels, who were described as having descended on the motel business and made it into their own. The article's provocative headline, "Indians Snap Up Small Motels," perhaps partly accounts for the virulent reaction it drew from two young white men with whom I was shooting some hoops that day on the basketball court adjoining the Arlington County Library in northern Virginia which I used to frequent since I first came to the U.S. with my parents in late 1976. These two young men were not doing too well on the court, and I have a vivid recollection that as they moved aggressively towards me, one of them snarled: "So you Indians want to take over. You better get out before I bash in your head." Some thirty years before this incident, a Patel had purchased a "motel," a word derived from "motor hotel," in California; and, as if on cue, he was followed by other Patels, and yet more Patels. The Patels in the United States, who originate largely from the Surat, Navsari, and Bulsar Districts of the state of Gujarat in western India, have their own amateur historian in the figure of Govind S. Bhakta, who in his short 2002 monograph on the Patels states that "approximately 40% of all U.S. motels are owned by Indian Americans." The industry's own estimates dating back to 1996 suggest more than 50 percent Indian ownership of all motels in the U.S., not only those at the lower end, and that figure may be considerably higher today. The vast bulk of these are owned by Gujaratis with surnames such as Patel, Bhakta, Desai, and Shah, and it is said that in smaller parts of America "Patel" is thought to be the Hindi word for motel.

The Patels have been the subject of dozens of newspaper articles and even doctoral dissertations. Govind Bhakta is one among several commentators to have profiled their history and documented their rise. By 1986, he points out, they were estimated to own 28 percent of 53,629 motels and small motels in the United States. However, though their success is a matter of much pride to the community and to other Indians, the more salient aspects of their history and its consequences for the study of the Indian diaspora in the United States have seldom been explored. Though Indians in the U.S. are generally studied in the aggregate, the history of the Patels illustrates the importance of kinship networks, marital alliances, language, residence patterns, gender roles, and family structure in understanding how migration takes place and why certain groups succeed where others may not or why they tend to predominate in certain professions. A third of all Indian immigrants to the United States are from Gujarat, and about five to six percent of Gujaratis are Patels. Accounting for about 1 percent of the Indian population, the Patels are, according to the Asian American Hotel Owners' Association Buying Guide, owners of about 90 to 95 percent of all Indian-owned motels. Moreover, the greater majority of Patels are employed in the motel business. Thus, in the first instance, the conditions of their success may be attributed to the fact that, utilizing the family reunification provisions of American immigration policy, Patels have consistently sponsored family members for immigration visas and eventual citizenship in the U.S., and that family members have been drawn into the business.

Since the story of the Patels has generally been told in the idiom of success, a slightly fuller sociological narrative of the "Patel Motel," more attentive to its cultural history and to the considerable hazards of the profession, is in order. The motel owner traditionally worked around the clock, had no retirement plan or health benefits, and could not conceive of the idea of a vacation—except that, when schools closed for vacation, he had good business at hand. He had to be constantly on guard for clients, visitors, and travelers who were determined to use the anonymity of the motel room to solicit sex for money, run drug deals, or seek refuge from the law. If the motelier blurred the distinction between work and vacation, the motel itself doubled as both workplace and home, as a liminal space between paid and unpaid work. Other family members, whose limited knowledge of English would have been something of a liability in the open market but was sufficiently good to man the front desk, could be employed to work around the motel, and though their labor was unpaid it was not unrecognized. The gender division of labor doubtless reinforced the subordinate role of women, but the motel also helped to pave the way for Indian American women to venture into the outer world.

The racism that Patels encountered as they struggled to find a niche for themselves in their new homeland was much less subtle than what was experienced by professional Indians. The aforementioned *Washington Post* article of 1979 quotes an anonymous broker from Virginia who told the reporter, "I don't like 'em. They haggle. They maneuver. They do things not customary in this country." Another described the Indians as possessed of "different business ethics," though one cannot doubt that "different" here is to be read much in the way in which Muslims are today habitually described as "different" from "us." If a motel advertised itself as "American owned," which many did, as even V.S. Naipaul observed in his journeys through the American South, it was more a statement that it was not owned by a Patel. The hotelier Gary Petitt, Chairman of Choice Hotels International, avers, "Patel meant the lowest end. People named Patel meant cooking in a curry pot and a kid getting her diapers changed on the counter, a poorly run hotel." That Mr. Petitt associated Patels and more generally Indians with curry should not wholly surprise us, considering that scores of narratives by second-generation Indian Americans still offer testimony of the overwhelming smell and memory of "curry" in their lives and their concern that curry had become a shorthand, in the American imagination, for Indians as alien and foreign. The young writer S. Mitra Kalita has written of her childhood years in Long Island, "Before friends came over, I sprayed several rounds of air freshener to rid our house of its pungent cooking odor; I never smelled the scent my brothers and I dubbed "IFS," for Indian Food Smell, but knew it existed because my classmates told me so."

What statements about curry-infested Patel motels disguise is an anxiety that a profoundly American institution, whose importance to the narrative of America as the ultimate space of freedom and mobility cannot be overstated, should have passed into the hands of those whose worldview, it is feared, has been shaped by an ethos dominated by constraints rather than liberty, boundedness rather than mobility. The motel lies in the space where people come and go, where the only history is the history that is made at the spur of the moment, where the automobile, that revered symbol of a permanent transitoriness, comes cruising in for the night. The motel is to American culture what the corner shop, so lovingly evoked in nineteenth-century English novels and popular culture as the social space where the last resistance to the mores of an encroaching industrial civilization could be staged, has been to English conceptions of Englishness. But when the motel, much like the corner shop in Britain, passed into the hands of Gujaratis, it also opened up the space for a new multiculturalism on the ground. The possibilities of this space, where Indians meet with African Americans, Mexicans, Nicaraguans, Salvadoreans, Koreans, and other immigrants, are far from having been fulfilled; but, nonetheless, the promise of a street-level or low-brow multiculturalism, at a great remove from the sanitized forms of multiculturalism that have been bequeathed by well-meaning liberals, aficionados of culture, and mandarins of the state, is one to which Indian Americans must hold.

It would be hard to find a business in the United States today that is so overwhelmingly dominated by one group. But if the narrative of the Patels, for all its fits and starts, appears to present a somewhat seamless history of an immigrant group finding its feet in the United States, then the history of the Asian American Hotel Owners Association (AAHOA), which today represents over 8,300 members owning more than 20,000 hotels with a million rooms and some 50 percent of economy lodging, suggests that this history is now moving into very different frontiers. "Asians have a rich tradition of entrepreneurship, self-improvement, and family values," says the web site of the organization [www.aahoa.com] with evidently a full awareness of how it might make itself attractive to an American audience. It adds that Indians started arriving in the U.S. "after India's independence" to pursue "their education and 'the American Dream,'" though no mention is made of the fact that the condition of their arrival was not only India's independence but legislation that no longer barred Indians from American shores. It is perhaps apposite that Indians, with their lavish traditions of hospitality, should now have conjoined hospitality to entrepreneurship and, in the land of business and success, have assisted in the birth of an industry. The hospitality industry was popular "because it offered immediate housing and cash flow," as well as the opportunity to integrate into American society. Many of the Gujaratis who moved into the motel business knew, one might say, a thing or two about mobility, integration, and (lack of) hospitality: exiled from East Africa, where they had put down roots over two to three generations before black nationalism rudely pushed them out of Uganda and Kenya, they imagined that in coming to the United States they had found a place that would be more hospitably inclined to their traditions of entrepreneurship, material advancement, and racial identity. But Indians, especially "those with the last name Patel," soon discovered that they faced resistance from bankers and insurance companies, and an organization, which eventually grew into the Indo-American Hospitality Association, was founded in 1985 in Tennessee to combat such discrimination. This organization merged in 1994 into the Asian American Hotel Owners Association (AAHOA), which had been founded in Atlanta in 1989, and the online history of the organization concludes with the observation that it is the "largest membership-based Indian business organization in the United States."

Just how is it that the association so effortlessly permits itself the conflation between "Asian" and "Indian"? The organization describes itself as an "Indian business organization," and the membership is exclusively Indian, indeed comprised largely of Patels with a sprinkling of other names. There is not the slightest hint of any wider consociation with Asian Americans, nor anything to suggest that "Asian American" is deployed strategically in the interest of forging closer links with other Asian Americans. It is more than likely that the multiple strands of Gujarati migration to the United States, from not only Gujarat but from East Africa and the United Kingdom where the designation "Asian" had long been associated with Indians, account in part for the nomenclature "Asian American" in AAHOA. Interestingly, some very recent chapters in the history of the AAHOA point to the simultaneous awareness among its members of its almost exclusively Indian and largely Gujarati membership, and a readiness on their part to proclaim in loud and clear terms their links to Gujarat and India.

At its annual meeting in March 2005, AAHOA sought to invite as its chief guest Narendra Modi, the Chief Minister of Gujarat. Modi is viewed with contempt and loathing by human rights advocates, liberals, and anyone who cares to be seen as adhering to progressive politics as a politician who permitted, perhaps even instigated, a pogrom against Muslims in Gujarat which took the lives of at least 2,000 Muslims and left another 150,000 or more homeless. AAHOA characterizes itself as a non-political organization, and its chief officials, when queried about their invitation to Modi, described him as a man who has opened up Gujarat to foreign investment from NRIs (non-resident Indians). They viewed the invitation to Modi to address the AAHOA annual convention as a good business proposition—for themselves and the state of Gujarat alike. Modi is a man who, in the view of his supporters, stands on the right side of development, unlike that other famous Gujarati, Mahatma Gandhi. Many Gujarati Hindus, in India and the U.S. alike, even describe Modi admiringly as a "Chota Sardar." Chota means small; Sardar, literally an overseer, boss, or big man, more significantly invokes memories of Sardar Vallabhai Patel, lionized as the "Iron Man of India," a major figure in the Indian nationalist movement who successfully integrated native states into India after the attainment of independence in 1947 and whose premature death in 1950 is still widely lamented by political realists as having robbed India of the services of a man who would have tamed Pakistan into submission.

Twenty-five, or even ten, years ago the AAHOA would not have sought to meddle into politics, or have had the self-confidence to associate with an openly political figure, much less one who is more sharply disliked among some Indians than any other contemporary Indian politician. But AAHOA did not envision that the invitation to Modi would be seen as an endorsement of a man accused of mass murder and crimes against humanity, or that today there are Indian American constituencies which can marshal resources in defense of a radical politics. Once the word had gone around on the internet, and academic and activist networks had been energized, the pressure upon AAHOA to retract the invitation mounted. Modi had been scheduled to appear on the popular cable talk show, Chris Matthew's *Hardball*; but that appearance was cancelled. Days before Modi was scheduled to arrive in the United States, the U.S. government took the unprecedented step of revoking his U.S. visa with a press release stating that American legislation did not permit the entry into the country of a person against whom there are serious allegations of criminal conduct and human rights violations. One of the many organizations that spearheaded the drive against Modi, and perhaps rightly claimed a hand in the U.S. State Department's decision to revoke his visa, is the Campaign Against Genocide (CAG). This organization, founded in early 2005, has no office and only a few core members, and its support base is comprised largely of Indian American academics, the vast majority of whom occupy professorships in history, anthropology, literature, cultural studies, and other disciplines in the humanities and softer social sciences at major colleges and universities.

Modi's supporters claimed that the U.S.-based Dalit Freedom Network, an organization which endeavors to provide India's most marginalized people all the opportunities for advancement available to other Indians, had worked in tandem with other anti-Indian groups such as CAG to diminish India's standing in the world, while Modi, in an interview with the popular Indian portal www.rediff.com, characterized the denial of the visa as an affront to all Indians. A few of CAG's members and supporters, all academics who have conjoined activism to their intellectual work, whipped up a storm in November 2002 when they published a report documenting the activities of the India Development and Relief Fund (IDRF), a non-profit Indian American organization which claims to do charitable work in India but is more likely supporting the work of organizations committed to Hindu nationalism and its pet projects, including religious education, *shuddhi* (purification and reconversion), and Hinduization of tribal populations. Nonetheless, the indubitable fact is that, in comparison with the AAHOA, which commands large financial resources and boasts a huge membership, the Campaign Against Genocide and other similar groups or organizations are miniscule in comparison, and it is a remarkable testament of their political astuteness that, cognizant of increased American sensitivities to the disrepute that people such as Modi can bring to the United States itself, they should have prevailed in the attempt to thwart Modi's American tour. On that same visit, Modi was scheduled to appear at California State University Long Beach (CSULB) and address a gathering at the inauguration of the

Yadunandan Center for India Studies, whose web site claims, as if to anticipate probable criticism, that it is "dedicated to the impartial study of India's cultures, peoples and history." The Yadunandan Center's Director and other senior CSULB officials, though advised by many Indian Americans to rescind their invitation to Modi, were not receptive to such suggestions; fortuitously, the cancellation of Modi's visa rendered any other protests unnecessary.

What the activities of the AAOA, the Yadunandan Center, and numerous other organizations underscore is something that is best described as *the politics of affluence and the anxiety of influence*. As Indian Americans become more established and affluent, they are keen that their presence should be registered not only in the political establishment but across large sectors of civil society; on the other hand, for all their affluence, Indian Americans have traditionally been afflicted by a huge anxiety of influence, an anxiety that only now, when news of India's rapid economic growth is splashed across the front pages of the *New York Times* and the cover of the *Economist*, shows some signs of diminishing. Though Indians could witness their ascendancy in American society, they did not see it translate into any increased visibility for themselves; indeed, the majority of them felt, not altogether incorrectly, that their ability to make their presence acknowledged corresponded to the visibility of India itself on the world stage. And, painful as it was to make such an admission, India had for something like five decades after independence from the British in 1947 been a largely inconsequential country, a mere speck on the American horizon—a shortcoming all the more shameful considering the size of the country, its huge population, and what many Indians held to be the unmatched accomplishments of Indian civilization.

Indian Americans were also rankled by what they took to be the tendency to treat Pakistan and India with parity, just as they smarted at the fact that communist China received far greater attention in the American press than democratic India. Throughout the 1980s and the first half of the 1990s, Indian Americans pondered how the United States, while claiming to be inspired by the ambition to spread democracy around the world, appeared to have little or no interest in cultivating the largest democracy in the world, a country whose steadfast resolution to adhere to democracy was all the more remarkable considering that it was something of an oasis in the large desert of authoritarian regimes, military dictatorships, and despotisms spread around the rest of South Asia, Latin America, and Africa. My own recollection of *desi* social gatherings during those decades is that one of the most frequent complaints was that news of India never made it to the television networks or the major newspapers, except when "hundreds" or, better still, "thousands" of Indians had died in religious violence, natural calamities, or man-made disasters such as some fatal train crash or the gas leak at Union Carbide's plant in Bhopal. Consequently, Indian Americans actively sought out signs that the United States was on the verge of recognizing India's potential greatness, or that India was not merely another country to be trampled upon at will. The rapid acceleration of the economy in very recent years has done a bit to diminish the anxiety of influence, as these headlines from *India-West*, the largest circulating weekly of its kind in California, amply suggest: "U.S. Acknowledging India's 'New Global Status'" (May 25, 2001); "Kissinger, a One-time Foe, Calls India a World Power" (November 12, 2004); and "[San Francisco-based] Asia Found[ation] Reiterates India's Rise as a Global Power" (November 26, 2004). Fantasies of India as a "global power" are disrupted neither by the grim reality that India continues to have by far the largest number of poverty-stricken people and illiterates nor by the recognition that the approbation of a war criminal is scarcely a badge of honor.

The growing affluence of Indian Americans has certainly emboldened them and made them willing to exercise their influence in all spheres of life. It will suffice to furnish a few illustrations, and one can reasonably commence with the emergence of philanthropy in Indian American communities. Though the greater majority of Indian Americans are still inclined to pour their wealth into the construction and management of temples, some have turned their attention to institutions back in India. A handful of the immensely wealthy Silicon Valley magnates, who perhaps marvel at the education they received at one of the Indian Institutes of Technology at state expense, have extended a helping hand to India's most famous set of institutions. Kanwal Rekhi, a graduate of IIT Bombay [now Mumbai], is among those who helped to establish The Indus Entrepreneurs (TiE) and the IIT Heritage Fund. He is lionized, for no apparent reason, in a recent book on diasporic Indian philanthropy as "a true living legend among the Indian Diaspora." There are also stories of heroic commoners who have committed their lives to some worthy social cause in India: to take one instance, New York taxi driver Om Dutt Sharma and his wife Krishna, a hospital nurse, have established with their meager savings a school in his native village in India for the daughters of farmers. Diasporic philanthropy, however, has many facets, and gift-giving is never without its politics. Some Indian Americans have begun to embrace the view that the responsibility to educate Americans, and indeed Indian Americans, about India and Indian traditions lies principally with them. The aforementioned Yadunandan Center in Long Beach, for instance, originated with a $200,000 donation from Uka Solanki, a Los Angeles-based Gujarati businessman who has made at least a minor fortune from a chain of grocery stores and has extended his patronage to other endeavors in the arts and education. Endowed chairs of Indian history or, more broadly, Indian studies have been inaugurated at nearly a dozen universities in less than a decade, among them Columbia, UCLA, Berkeley, UC Santa Barbara, UC Santa Cruz, and Indiana University.

One might reasonably argue that, in endowing university chairs or helping to promote Indian studies on American campuses, Indian Americans are merely doing what many other ethnic groups with affluence have long been doing. Indian Americans have come late to philanthropy: not only are cultural traditions of gift-giving implicated, but there is some awareness that the resolute focus on temple-building and other religious activities may have been detrimental to the advancement of the community's political interests. However, as I have already suggested, the feeling that India is entitled to much greater respect than the country was traditionally accorded persists, and Indian Americans do not doubt that a more enhanced place for India in the world political order will perforce lead to renewed respect for themselves. The debate over the constitution of the UN Security Council furnishes a good illustration of some of these points. Until nearly the end of 2005, when reform and expansion of the Security Council was still a topic of some discussion in the media, Indian Americans took it upon themselves to assist India in its quest for a permanent seat in the Security Council. The U.S.-India Political Action Committee initiated an online petition in support of India's bid for permanent membership with the observation that it is an "ancient civilization," occupies a strategic location in Asia, is demonstrating impressive growth, and has played a critical role in the non-proliferation of nuclear weapons. Mukesh Advani, President of the Northern California-based South Asian Bar Association, went on record as saying that India's case for permanent membership had been made by the country's "vast pool of technicians and scientists," its "huge strides in the Space technologies," and its status in the "third world" as a country providing "moral leadership." This specious argument, which for a moment does not consider other, more ethical, alternatives to the strong-arm politics enshrined in the idea of the Security Council, is little more than a diasporic campaign for the idea, with which the Bharatiya Janata Party sought to win the 2004 election, of "India Shining."

Alongside these attempts to increase India's visibility and improve the country's standing in the world are a large spate of activities designed to diminish if not eliminate the jaundiced and ignorant views which, so many Indian Americans allege, have diminished the esteem in which Hinduism might otherwise have been held. If I have here moved from the anxiety of political influence which pervades Indian American life to the anxieties experienced by Hindus upon the practice of their faith, it is emphatically not because I view "Indian" and "Hindu" as synonymous terms, or even forming something of a natural continuum. Quite to the contrary, it is imperative that the frequent elision from Indian to Hindu be subjected to rigorous scrutiny and critique; simultaneously, it is unquestionable that the Hindus among Indian Americans feel, so to speak, twice-afflicted. In this respect, nothing is perhaps as interesting as the interventions of a group that styles itself as "American Hindus Against Defamation," more generally known by its acronym, AHAD. Its baseline position is that the obscurity surrounding Hinduism, an allegedly mysterious religion of many gods and strange rituals, has rendered the religion and its adherents more vulnerable, and that the protections available to the more organized monotheistic faiths are unavailable to the adherents of a religion which has no history of proselytization. AHAD is vigorous in the pursuit of its ambition to make those who would demean or slight the Hindu faith, or mock traditions and tenets of belief which Hindus view as sacrosanct, accountable to Hindus. AHAD has conducted campaigns, through word of mouth, print media, and the internet, to extract apologies from American Eagle Outfitters for marketing flip flops with images of the Hindu god Ganesh on the sole; the toilet seat manufacturer Sittin' Pretty for placing images of Shiva, Kali, and Ganesh on toilet seat covers; the kitchen and bath appliances company Kohler for modeling a scantily-clad woman after the dancing form of Shiva (Nataraj); the West Coast microbrewery Lost Coast for putting Ganesh on one of their pale ales; and so on.

The veneration of Hindu deities is a subject on which one might entertain many and often deliciously contradictory thoughts, but the point that an image of a god on underwear or a bottle of alcohol would be deeply wounding to most Hindu sensibilities is beyond dispute. Many a sensitive soul has been stirred to action at perceived insults to one's religion, though it is far from clear that Hindu sympathies lay unequivocally with Muslims who were recently outraged at the Danish cartoons which had taken some liberties with Muslim religious beliefs. I have heard it often said, and internet discussions in chat rooms confirm this impression, that Muslims are "unusually" sensitive in such matters. The softer version of this view is that so much is forbidden to Muslims that offending their sensibilities requires little by way of imagination, effort, or thought. But, as far as Hindu sensibilities are in question, the matter is not so easily closed. Rohinton Mistry's novel, *Such a Long Journey*, suggests that humor should never be overlooked as a way of ameliorating a community's concerns. An older resident of a neighborhood hits upon an ingenious scheme to prevent men from urinating against a nearby wall and so filling the air with a revolting stench: he hires a pavement painter, upon whose images of gods and goddesses people shower money, to whitewash the urine-drenched well and paint on it, in true ecumenical fashion, a string of Hindu gods and goddesses alongside such revered religious figures as the Buddha, Christ, and Mahavira. And there is still the more pressing question: just what exactly is defamation, and if it is a strictly legal category, has Hinduism itself ever entertained any conception of "defamation"? One might legally blaspheme Christianity, as in Britain, but can one be blasphemous as such in speaking of Hinduism?

It is also instructive that American Hindus Against Defamation does not confine its attention solely to religious insults. One of their more aggressive campaigns was mounted, though apparently not with any success, against a toy manufacturer that has marketed a series of seven "Trash Talker Dolls" [www. trashtalkerdolls.net]. "Mr. Patel" was issued in 2004: the fidelity to detail is obviously of little importance, since a man on whose head sits a large white turban is unlikely to have a bindi on his forehead, and certainly Gujarati men do not sport such a countenance. With a click of a button, "Mr. Patel" utters one of five programmed sentences. AHAD's activists were evidently not pleased by the sentence, "Hamburger. Everything on its please, but no beef," though one suspects that many, Indians not excluded, would be tickled pick by such humor. Insofar as vegetarianism is to some Hindus and many Jains an article of religious belief, AHAD seems very much to have been opposing the insult to their religious sensibilities. However, vegetarianism leads to no reduction of appetite for sex; if anything, the vegetarian may be overcompensating with a renewed libido. This is only one of many offensive insinuations, alongside the Gujarati's alleged incapacity to master the idioms of the English language, on offer in Mr. Patel's other utterance: "I am needing to want sex with you now."

One might predictably posit first amendment rights against the widely accepted cultural and social mores of modern democracies, which insist on respect for other cultures and deplore ethnic and racial stereotyping. Such debates are bound to remain inconclusive; but, most pertinently, AHAD's pronouncements lead to the inescapable feeling that the organization's supporters view their religion as one that is especially vulnerable. AHAD's web site states, apropos of Sittin' Pretty's toilet covers, that "little did [Hindus] know there is no limit to how low one can sink when it comes to the depiction of revered Hindu images" [www.hindunet.org/anti_defamation]. The world has trampled over Hindus much too long, AHAD has often argued, and it aims to extract apologies from offenders. Little does AHAD know that an epidemic of apologies engulfs the world, and that the apology has become one of the latest contrivances by which the West seeks to assert its moral superiority over the rest of the world.

The Landscapes of Representation in Internet Modernity

With the dramatic growth of the Indian American population, the cultures and technologies of representation available to members of the community have likewise become more complex and diverse. Indian Americans have begun to understand that old Marxian adage: those who cannot represent themselves are condemned to be represented by others, and they are equally condemned to live someone else's conception of their own lives. Whether or not Indian Americans stand at the vanguard of internet modernity, they are doubtless permanent residents of cyberland. The last two decades have also witnessed an explosion of Indian and more broadly South Asian print media, the emergence of community-based NGOs, political organizations, and women's groups, the growing presence of Indian Americans among the professoriate in not merely the sciences, medicine, engineering, and business schools but in the humanities and social sciences, and the public celebration of an Indian American literature. The attempt to project an "India Shining," the campaign name by which the ruling Hindu nationalist party in 2004 sought to attract voters, has certainly increased the country's stock in the United States, and this accumulation of cultural capital can be gauged by an array of social and cultural phenomena, from the auctioning of Indian art at previously unheard of sums of money at Sotheby's to the "India Now" Film Festival at the Museum of Modern Art projected for April 2007. A brief glance at some of these developments can do much to elucidate the contemporary histories of Indian Americans.

I had previously adverted to the Campaign Against Genocide (CAG), which is described as a coalition of thirty-five organizations but in its operations is a very small organization whose "membership" is drawn from the ranks of such of those academics who are more hospitably disposed towards public work and activism than is commonly the case among the professoriate. The group came together in early 2005, and some of its leading activists were among those who had worked together on the "Campaign to Stop Funding Hate," tracing in effect the route taken by American dollars as they wound up in the hands of militant Hindu groups in India. One of the less recognized aspects of these campaigns is the fact that twenty years ago, one would have been relatively hard pressed to find more than a handful of Indian American academics who had not gravitated towards the physical sciences, engineering, medicine, and other well-paying professions, and even fewer who were drawn to some form of political engagement. While the inclination to enter into one of these professions has scarcely disappeared, the ranks of Indian American graduate students and faculty who are strongly committed to humanistic education and to the university as the twin site of intellectual practices and as a space of dissent have steadily grown. Though the Indian American academics who have gained the most visibility in the humanities and the social sciences are not generally among those who have been most committed to public activism, the campaigns garnered wide support among Indian American academics across the country. The signature campaigns, which characterize internet modernity as much as anything else, also show how Indian American scholars are now dispersed throughout the gargantuan American academy. Indeed, there is hardly a department of English at a major liberal arts college, or state or private university, which does not have on its faculty roster at least one Indian American. Academics such as the cultural anthropologist Arjun Appadurai, the literary theorist Homi Bhabha, and the multi-faceted Gayatri Chakravorty Spivak are not only among the most prominent Indian Americans in the country, but holders of endowed professorships at the country's most elite universities who occupy besides a leading role in their own disciplines.

Both Bhabha and Spivak, for all their interventions, also have unenviable reputations as wielders of some of the most dense and obscurantist prose in the English language. Though widely celebrated in the academy, most Indian American scholars have made little attempt to reach out to a wider public, and few of them have ever written for the mainstream American press or even in other publications with something of a wide reach. The most obvious exception is Amartya Sen, who occupied a professorship at Harvard before taking up the Mastership of Trinity College at Cambridge; he has since returned to Harvard, and has become something like the supreme spokesman for a certain liberal conception of the world to which many people are prepared to give their assent. If Indian American scholars have been reticent in writing for popular journals and newspapers, we might say that Amartya Sen, whose Nobel Prize in Economics has earned him a sacrosanct place in the middle-class imagination of Indians (in India and abroad), compensates for their deficiencies by venturing to give forth opinions on every conceivable subject across a wide range of publications.

Outside the academic world, writing in idioms and genres more congenial to a wider audience, Indian American novelists and poets have created a significant and even distinct niche for themselves. For decades, the only modern Indian or Indian American writers known to American audiences were R.K. Narayan, Ved Mehta, and V.S. Naipaul. Mehta had arrived in the U.S. to attend a school for blind children in Arizona, and his gift for writing earned him a regular and highly coveted spot in the *New Yorker*. Almost nothing ever disturbed the placid tone in which Mehta wrote, and no great passions animated him, unless it be the lives of Daddyji, Mummyji, Chachaji, and Auntyji. No two writers perhaps offered such a contrast as Narayan and Naipaul: where the former struck a remarkable note of congeniality, and abided by a gentle sense of humor and irony, Naipaul wrote with seething contempt about "Third World" societies and in particular India, from where his father had fled for Trinidad. Only two Indian writers of any great distinction were settled in the United States, Raja Rao and G.V Desani—the former, a novelist's novelist, had only a small following and remained wholly unknown to American audiences, while Desani, whose *All About H. Hatterr* (1948) suggested a dexterity and playfulness with the language that few postmodernists have been able to emulate, had obviously penned a magnum opus after which all labor was bound to look superfluous. Neither had written about the Asian Indian experience, or even a novel on American society. Both writers died in obscurity recently.

By contrast, contemporary Indian writers command recognition, and advances from publishers that would make some Silicon Valley entrepreneurs and venture capitalists envious. Salman Rushdie, one might say, is Amartya Sen's counterpart in the world of literary celebrities: though he relocated to the United States in the aftermath of the September 11 bombings, he now speaks of New York as if it had always been his home. His shorter opinion pieces and essays nearly advert to the U.S. as the last beacon of hope for humankind, and he has joined the chorus of voices who are firm in their conviction that the freedoms for which the U.S. stands are under relentless assaults by Muslim zealots. None of Rushdie's major novels is, however, set in the U.S.—and the country occupies a similarly marginal existence in the writings of the novelist and cultural anthropologist Amitav Ghosh, who uniquely straddles both the literary and academic worlds. Vikram Seth, after his magisterial attempt at the great California novel, *The Golden Gate* (1986), written as 690 tetrameter sonnets, quit America—both as an abode and in his writings. Thus, though Asian Indian writers are now prominent in the American literary scene, it is far from certain that they have so far contributed to American literature as such, or helped to shape and mold it in significantly new ways. One is thus also justified in asking whether they should be viewed as Asian Indian writers, or simply as Indian writers who deploy a near global language in a world of complex transnational exchanges and interconnected histories. Oddly enough, while the world's gaze is turned towards New York, one of the city's more celebrated Indian Americans, the writer Suketu Mehta, has spun together a large narrative about that other city, Bombay. Does not the American setting interest Mehta, or for that matter the novelist Vikram Chandra, whose *Death and Longing in Bombay* (1997) has been followed by a paean to that city called *Sacred Games* (2006), or should we read their works as informed by a particular diasporic sensibility?

Asian Indian writing is nonetheless much more variegated than was possible even a decade ago, and some of it is on witness in recent initiatives, such as DesiLit, which describes itself as a group "building support for South Asian and diasporic writing" [desilit.org]. The group is forming chapters throughout the U.S. and commenced an online magazine, *DesiLit Magazine*, in 2006. The novel requires, perhaps, a different grounding in the social order, an intimacy which is not so easily granted. That may be one reason why at least male Indian American novelists have not generally been able to set their stories to American life, while writers working in other literary forms have perhaps been more successful in breaching the borders. Shishir Kurup, a talented playwright in the Los Angeles area, has sought to understand how the worldview of the Indian epics might be introduced in a secular society running on homogenous time. What might a Ramayana for the United States of America look like, and what *puranic* forms can best capture the life forms of American culture? Writing somewhat in the tradition of John Berger, who has the gift of turning the life of a country doctor in Britain into a parable about the ethics of compassion, care, and conviviality in a society driven by speed, the doctor Abraham Verghese has penned a poignant narrative on AIDS in small-town America. The young Atul Gawande, a surgeon by vocation and a writer by avocation, is perhaps poised to step into the shoes of Oliver Sacks.

And yet, some fifteen years before Verghese or Gawande, Agha Shahid Ali was, in his own manner, juxtaposing multiple landscapes, ruminating on the exilic life that thoughtful people must often lead. Shahid, as he was known to friends, colleagues, and readers of his work, was brought up in Kashmir and Delhi before he moved to the U.S. to attend college. He seems forever to have lived with the pain of Kashmir, and at one moment in 1996 described himself as a "Kashmiri American Kashmiri." Shahid's collections of verse—*The Half Inch Himalayas* (1987); *A Nostalgist's Map of America* (1991); *The Country Without a Post Office* (1997); and *Rooms Are Never Finished* (2001)—invoke a cartography of longing, memory, and exile. *A Nostalgist's Map of America* traverses the landscapes of the American West, and is sandwiched between his recollections of Kashmir, much as Shahid found himself caught between India and America. Shahid, in *The Country Without a Post Office*, might well have been describing himself, a man without a country. The last collection was published in the year of his premature death; it is prescient in its anticipation of death and the unfinished task of the writer. Kashmir was never far from his mind; but *pari passu* every recollection of Kashmir, what the Mughal Emperor Babur described as a "paradise on earth," is also tinged with an awareness of the discourse of America as another site of paradise. Shahid's poetry maps America on to Kashmir, Kashmir on to America, an answer as well to the dominant voices of exceptionalism that have informed our understandings of both societies.

It is perhaps not accidental that the writings of Asian Indian women writers, among them Bharati Mukherjee, Meena Alexander, Jhumpa Lahiri, and the largely young members of the Berkeley South Asian women collective who co-authored *Our Feet Walk the Sky* (1993), speak more directly to the condition of being an Indian in the United States. As has been the case with many immigrant groups, the men came first—both in the first phase of immigration from the late 1890s to 1924, as well as in the first couple of decades following the passage of INS legislation in 1965. Whereas the men could create a niche for themselves outside the home, particularly in the professions, the women came largely as brides. Chitra Divakaruni has acquired a huge following among young Indian American women with stories of arranged marriages and repressed sexuality, the pressures placed upon women to conform to notions of Indian culture and family, the loneliness of the housewife, and the desire of Indian American women to create lives of their own. Many critics charge Divakaruni with playing up to the stereotypes of Indian women as submissive that predominate in the wider culture, and it has been argued that a surprisingly monolithic view of Indian American women emerges from her writings. However, if Alexander, Lahiri, and Divakaruni resonate so strongly with Indian American women, they do so partly because of a profound unwillingness in the community to question the sanctimonious pieties about allegedly model Indian American families. The rate of heterosexual marriage is higher in the Indian American community than for any other racial or ethnic group; at the same time, as social workers have amply documented, Indian American women are more likely than women of most other ethnic groups to be subjected to domestic violence, sexual abuse, and other forms of exploitation. Over the last fifteen years, numerous women's help groups and shelters—Apna Ghar, Saheli, Narika, Sahara, and Maitri—have sprung up in metropolitan centers. If Indian Americans stood to profit by the hard-won achievements of the civil rights movement, then one should expect, as well, that the feminist movement in the United States has been inspiring for some Indian American women.

Even as Indian American voices have now been added to that vast canvas known as American literature, it remains an open question to what extent such voices, even allowing for their cascading effect in the future, will appreciably alter the main contours of American literature. Are these voices instances of additive literature, contributing to the celebratory conception of multicultural America, likely to alter the fundamental ideas of what constitutes "America"? Still, there is little doubt that Indian American literature has arrived with something of a splash, quite unlike the rather quiet place occupied by South Asian American print media in American journalism. An earlier chapter detailed the history of the Ghadr movement and its flagship publication, and a more comprehensive account of Indian print media in the U.S. would have to extend attention to such periodicals as *Independent Hindustan*, which commenced publication in 1920 and advocated Indian independence within the broad framework of an anti-imperialist struggle, and *India Bulletin*, the organ of the Friends of India similarly dedicated to the promotion of the emancipation of India from British rule.

The modern period of Indian print journalism in the U.S. dates back to 1970, when Gopal Raju brought out *India Abroad* as a monthly, though its success prompted him to transform it into a fortnightly, and soon thereafter weekly, publication. *India Abroad* was the only forum for Indian American expression throughout the 1970s, somewhat alleviating the loneliness of a community still searching for its place in American society, and it has retained its standing as the most prestigious of South Asian publications down to the present day. In recent years, however, the South Asian American print media has burgeoned, and Indian grocery stores are the outlets where one is most likely to pick up a copy of *Indian Reporter and World News*, *India Bulletin, India Tribune*, *Desi Talk*, *India Post*, *India Journal*, *India West*, and many other publications, some even in Punjabi, Gujarati, Urdu and other South Asian languages. Allied Media Corp., which describes itself as a business specializing in "multicultural communication," catering to various ethnic markets and enclaves, lists close to fifty South Asian periodicals serving the Indian-American, Pakistani-American, and Bangladeshi-American communities on its web site [www.allied-media.com]. If one had to hazard the broadest generalization about how Indian American print media in particular has changed over the last decade, one might aver both that it displays a greater degree of confidence in the idea that South Asians now have a permanent and enduring home in the U.S., and that the general affluence of the community permits it to indulge its interests in fashion, entertainment, holidaying, and what might be described as "lifestyle choices."

More recent publications, all started in the last few years, include *Rivaaj*, dedicated to bringing to "center stage the positive achievements, tastes, and styles of South Asian Americans;" *Anokhi*, modeled after glossy newsstand magazines such as *Vogue* and *Vanity Fair*, and featuring on one of its recent issues a cover article called "India Goes Global and Woos the Sultry and Sexy In You;" and *iStyle*, which purports to be "a *unique* fashion and lifestyle magazine that caters specifically to the North American South Asian woman" but in actuality strings together the most predictable clichés in its endeavor, as the Allied Media web site states, to "fuse both cultures, Eastern and western, to fit our own sense of style and identity." More remarkable still is *Nirvana Woman*, which admits that it targets "affluent, dynamic and upscale college and professional Indian-American women," and signals its impression that Indian American women are no longer a group of people who can be ignored with the further observation that the magazine "is now available nationally in major bookstores including Barnes & Noble and Borders, and many metro airports." There is, in all this, the now-familiar idea that no barriers exist to restrict women in their upward march, and that South Asian women, much like white women, can lay claim to the world as their own and even enjoy it. The spiritual and material conceptions of Nirvana can coexist peacefully. The East-West blend has more lives than a cat.

Though Allied Media, pointing to the huge disposable incomes in South Asian households and recognizing that "Asian Indian Americans are one of the more affluent, well-educated and well-informed online ethnic communities in the United States," makes a strong case for an ethnic press, second-generation Indian Americans show every sign of veering towards a more cyber-oriented conception of the cultural and political life. I have elsewhere written extensively on the marked tendency displayed by Hinduism's adherents in the United States to turn towards various forms of digital media, and in particular the internet, to forge new forms of Hindu identity, furnish Hinduism with a purportedly more coherent and monotheistic form, engage in debates on American multiculturalism, and partake of the protocols of citizenship in the digital age. While it is certainly possible to argue that adherents of Hinduism are not alone in being predisposed towards digital media, and there are at present no comparative studies that might enable us to gauge internet usage among different religious communities, there is an overwhelming amount of anecdotal and circumstantial evidence to suggest that Hindus have been particularly conscientious, if not innovative and aggressive, in mobilizing members of the perceived Hindu community through the internet. Only Hinduism, if one may put it so boldly, can match the internet's playfulness: the religion's "330 million" gods and goddesses, a testimony to the intrinsically decentered and polyphonic nature of the faith, find correspondence in the world wide web's multiple points of origin, intersection, and dispersal. Moreover, as I documented at great length in some of my earlier work, the rise of Hindu militancy in India since the late 1980s, signaled by the term Hindutva (the "essence" of Hinduism), had its counterpart in the creation of new Hindutva histories on the internet. These public histories, which have been wholly discredited by scholars of Indian history, have nonetheless been received with wide approbation by Hindus settled in the United States. As I have sought to establish, Indian American Silicon Valley engineers, and thousands of Indian male graduate students in the computer sciences, labored over websites dedicated to revisionist and Hindu nationalist accounts of Indian history and culture and generated, by the early 1990s, various listserves and bulletin boards such as alt.hindu and soc.culture.indian.

To understand the politics of the internet's deployment by nationalist Hindus who are fully cognizant of the discourses of multiculturalism, and the opposition they have aroused among secular and avowedly progressive Hindus, one can perhaps turn profitably to the fierce controversy that arose in California in 2005–2006 when certain Hindus, availing themselves of the six-year review of world history textbooks for sixth- and seventh-graders mandated by the State Board of Education, proposed over 200 changes to portions of the text pertaining to ancient Indian history and Hinduism. They argued, for instance, that Hinduism should be represented as a monotheistic rather than polytheistic faith, and they vigorously averred that in ancient India men had not more rights than women, a claim encountered in these texts, but rather that men and women had "different" rights. Though scholarly communities engaged in ancient Indian history, comparative linguistics, Indo-European studies, and comparative religion are nearly unanimous in holding to the view that there were Aryan migrations to India commencing around 1500 BC (and perhaps somewhat earlier), the Hindus who agitated for the changes claim that India is the original homeland of the Aryans.

Led by the Hindu Education Foundation and the Vedic Foundation, both organizations based in the United States, Indian American Hindus waged, predominantly over the internet, a relentless campaign to energize the Hindu community into action. The California State Board of Education reported, throughout late 2005 and early 2006, being flooded with emails, faxes, letters, and phone calls from irate Hindus who claimed that textbook representations of Hinduism and the caste system were calculated to make Indian American schoolchildren feel ashamed about their faith and heritage, and that in multicultural America Hindus are entitled to as much respect as adherents of any other religion or community. As is now widely known, the proposed alterations to the textbooks would have been implemented but for the last-minute "awakening" of scholars of Indian history, of Indian origin and otherwise, who were in agreement that many, though not all, of the proposed changes could not be justified. Several internet campaigns—one among fifty renowned scholars of Indology from around the world, the other among South Asian scholars in the humanities and social sciences at leading American universities, and one waged by secular activists, progressives, and Hindus who disputed that the advocates of Hindutva could speak for all Hindus, not to mention other Indians—eventually led the State Board, at two contentious meetings, to reject the most controversial of the alterations proposed by those acting in the name of the Hindu community.

In the textbooks controversy, a number of important issues come to the fore as we attempt to understand the rules of civic engagement and the protocols of citizenship in the digital age. It is not surprising that, as India slowly begins to emerge as an Asian power, the Hindu community in the United States, which contributes substantially more to direct foreign investment in India than Hindus elsewhere, should begin to feel emboldened, mindful of its "rights" and prerogatives; nor is it surprising that these Hindus should view themselves as the vanguard of what I would characterize as revolutionary internet Hinduism. The internet is not merely the medium through which debates on Hinduness and Indianness are being conducted, it is the vehicle, nowhere more so than among Indian Americans, for advancing a new conception of Hinduism as a global faith. If internet Hindutva's proponents had their way, Hinduism, or more precisely Hindutva, would have something of an ummah, a worldwide community that would also assist in bringing pliant Hindus, both in India and in the older Indian diasporas of the nineteenth century, to an awareness of the global strengths of a "modern" Hindu community. These forms of political participation, however, also give rise to other considerations scarcely addressed in the literature. Though nationalist Hindus in the United States take recourse to arguments about multiculturalism, they have not at all been hospitable to multiculturalism or even Indian variants of pluralism in India itself. One also wonders whether increased internet mobilization of the Indian American Muslim community might have done something to mitigate the pogrom against Muslims in the Indian state of Gujarat in 2002. Finally, it is necessary to ask what rules of civic engagement might easily be broken by internet citizenship, and what rules, if any, internet citizenship can bring to political discussions. As the following chapter suggests, there are many other interfaces for articulations of citizenship in a world where rules of civic engagement are evidently still under negotiation.

Politics & the Future of
Indians in the United States

Scholars of diasporic communities have long been cognizant
of the fact that an immigrant community generally retains a
complex, even torturous, relationship with the "homeland."
The term NRI, or Non-resident Indian, was originally devised to refer to Indians settled in the United States, and more
broadly in the affluent industrialized nations, even though
older, and larger, Indian communities were to be found in
Mauritius, Trinidad, South Africa, and other nations. It was
always understood, though never formally acknowledged,
that NRIs were to be placed in a different category than the
descendants of indentured laborers, and the Government of
India foolishly ratified this openly discriminatory understanding when it proposed, in 2004, to confer the right of dual citizenship only upon Indians settled in certain countries such
as the United States and Australia. For their part, Indian
Americans have displayed an increasing interest in exercising
their influence to make India more hospitable to foreign investment, and over the years they have successfully prevailed
upon the Indian government to rescind regulations that forbid

NRIs from owning property in India. One is now beginning to see even more complex manifestations of the Indian American encounter with the homeland. The brain drain, it has been suggested, is being reversed: not only do several thousand Indian Americans return to India each year, but they take back capital, entrepreneurial skills, and technical know-how. As we might recall, among the beneficiaries in India of American philanthropy have been the famous Indian Institutes of Technology, some of whose millionaire graduates, even when they do not return to the homeland, have laid their wealth at the mother's bosom.

What is rather more striking, perhaps, is the manner in which the internal politics of the Indian subcontinent is echoed in the politics of South Asian communities in the United States. When a portion of Chicago's Devon Avenue, a six-block "desi" stretch of which houses the usual assortment of "Patel Brothers" grocery stores, jewelers, Indian restaurants, Bollywood music and film outlets, and 220-volt appliance and sari stores, was renamed after Gandhi, the Pakistani businesses successfully applied pressure to have an adjoining section named after Jinnah, the founder of Pakistan. From the standpoint of Indian Americans, at least, this is illustrative of the tendency in the Pakistani American community to insist upon parity, as though Jinnah, who is virtually unknown outside Pakistan, were a world-historical figure comparable to Gandhi. The official view of multiculturalism may leave local officials no choice but to comply with such requests, if only to ensure that one community is not viewed as receiving favors from the state while other communities are ignored, but Indian Americans remain convinced that the United States has coddled Pakistan for much too long.

Much more dramatic, and rife with consequences, is the support rendered to various political movements in India among their adherents in the United States. The Sikh separatist movement in the Punjab, which aimed at creating an autonomous homeland for the Sikhs to be known as Khalistan, received much institutional and financial support from Sikh militants in the United States, Canada, and Britain, and one of its most vociferous advocates, the late Jagjit Singh Chauhan, even set up in London a Khalistan government in exile, issuing passports, currency, and other paraphernalia that mark a nation-state. Khalistanis in the U.S. exuded confidence, even arrogance, certain that the irrepressible Dan Burton, who has represented Indiana in the House of Representatives since 1982, would every now and then issue a harangue against human rights atrocities in India and press for an American reprimand of the Indian state. Remarkably, though not surprisingly, the demand for Khalistan continued to flourish among certain Sikh communities in the U.S. even after it had become greatly attenuated in India itself.

The Council of Khalistan, still based in Washington, has a new Congressional supporter in Edolphus Towns (New York), and Representative Towns periodically inserts statements in the *Congressional Record* denouncing India for atrocities against minorities. On February 24, 2004, in the 108th Congress, Towns furnished a number of "250,000 Sikhs" as having been killed owing to repression by the Indian state. But, as by far the greater number of Sikhs settled in the U.S. now recognize, the struggle for recognition must move in other directions and principally demands an engagement with American politics and society. In the immediate wake of 9/11, when assaults against Muslims and Sikhs were widely reported, there was much greater awareness among American Sikhs about the desirability of combating the widespread ignorance about Sikh history and religion in the U.S. The Sikh advocacy group SALDEF (Sikh American Legal Defense and Education Fund), which commenced operations in 1996 as the Sikh Media Advisory and Research Taskforce (SMART), has done exemplary work in this regard, seeking to sensitize all Americans, and in particular state agencies, about Sikh faith and history, the right of Sikhs to wear a turban to work, and the use of the kirpan or ceremonial dagger [see www.saldef.org]. SMART holds training workshops for state and local officials, employers, and civil rights groups.

What Khalistan was to Sikhs, it is sometimes said, Kashmir is to South Asian Muslims. Kashmir is certainly the foreign policy issue about which South Asian Muslims feel most strongly and where opinion is most divided. Apart from Pakistan, which has installed a lobbying machinery in Washington, various political organizations keep up the pressure for some resolution to "the Kashmir problem." Pamphlets, resolutions, speeches, and literature drawing attention to human rights violations by the Indian state, and calling for a political solution, are very much part of the business of the day—and, precisely for that reason, of no huge consequence. The New Jersey-based Association of Pakistani Professionals, to take one organization, even works at the state level, and it has expressed pleasure at its recent triumph in New Hampshire, where the state legislature recently voted to urge the U.S. Congress to hold hearings on Kashmir. Among Indian American Muslims, and indeed among Kashmiri Americans themselves, there is much ambivalence. Though in principle most people agree that self-determination for Kashmiris would be the most desirable outcome, it is also widely recognized that this solution is precisely the one that is least amenable to India, Pakistan, and even the United States, which views itself as having enough trouble on its hands with Muslim militancy in Pakistan and Afghanistan and fears that an independent Kashmir would become yet another haven for "Muslim terrorists" and a conduit for the illegal trafficking of arms, ammunition, and a variety of "weapons of mass destruction."

Some Indian American Muslims are outright opposed to Kashmir's assimilation into Pakistan: they recognize that Kashmir, as the only Muslim majority state in India, serves as something of a litmus test for Indian democracy, and that the loss of Kashmir to Pakistan, scarcely a state which can be described as a model of democratic pluralism, might lead to an erosion of the civil, social, and political rights of Muslims in India. The Kashmiri Pandits, the other victims in the battles between militants and state forces, have also become more vocal and created a "Virtual Homeland for Kashmiri Pandits." In recent years, the nuclearization of the subcontinent, the "war on terror," and even India's rapid economic growth have appreciably altered the political considerations which used to reign supreme. The precarious state of Pakistan has dampened the enthusiasm with which some South Asian, especially Indian, Muslims might previously have contemplated the idea of Kashmir's absorption into Pakistan. On the other hand, notwithstanding the pogrom carried out against Muslims in Gujarat in 2002, there is some feeling that economic advancement, conjoined with setbacks for Hindu nationalist parties, points to a more robust future for Muslims in India. Indeed, the Indian Muslim Council–U.S.A has pledged itself to a more ecumenical conception of political intervention, and states on its web site that it is dedicated to the task of "safeguarding India's pluralist and tolerant ethos" [http://www.imc-usa.org]. On the question of the atrocities perpetrated against Muslims in Gujarat, for instance, it rightfully took a strong stand and insistently pressed for the perpetrators of the violence to be brought to trial.

Support for Hindu militancy, and more broadly the vigorous even aggressive affirmation of pride in Hindu culture, have taken many forms. I have previously adverted to some instances, though many more easily come to mind. It is a matter of public record that some Hindus took out full page ads in Indian American publications extolling Hindus in India who were firmly committed to the agitation surrounding the Babri Masjid, a sixteenth-century mosque in Ayodhya that was claimed by militants to have been built on the foundation of a Hindu temple. The mosque was eventually destroyed by Hindu militants on December 6, 1992. The Chicago chapter of the VHP unabashedly celebrated the "thunderous successful culmination" of the "liberation" of Ayodhya from the centuries-old tyranny of Muslim rule and welcomed "the dawn of Hindu Rashtra" [nation]. Indian American Hindus have poured much money into the construction of a projected grand new Hindu temple in Ayodhya, and contribute generously to the activities of the Vishwa Hindu Parishad (VHP) and Rashtriya Swayamsevak Sangh (RSS), though often this money is channeled into sister organizations that claim non-profit status.

That the ossified Hinduism of some Hindus in the United States, who are far removed from the complexities of the faith and its rich engagement with the multiple strands of Indian civilization, has unsavory political ramifications is nowhere better illustrated than in the activities of the Los Angeles-based Federation of Hindu Associations (FHA). Instituting a "Hindu of the Year" award in 1994, the FHA at once conferred it jointly upon Bal Thackeray and Sadhvi Ritambara, two stalwarts of the Hindutva movement who have warned Indian Muslims that they must be prepared to live in India on terms dictated by the Hindu community or should leave for Pakistan or some other predominantly Muslim land. The Gujarati Hindu community in the U.S. is so heavily communalized that few of its members had the courage to condemn unequivocally the killing of Muslims in Gujarat; on the contrary, Narendra Modi is feted in Gujarati American households, and spoken of with great pride as the inheritor of the legacy of Sardar Patel. In interviews conducted with some twenty-fve members of the Gujarati community in the Los Angeles area over the summer of 2005, one view was repeatedly encountered: Modi is a good politician, competent, incorruptible, business-friendly, one of a rare breed of politicians who will stand up to pseudo-secularists and not accept any nonsense from minorities.

It is ironical, considering that the killings of Gujarati Muslims scarcely raised a stir in the wider Hindu community in the U.S., that some Hindus have even put into place institutional mechanisms for monitoring the violations of the human rights of Hindus. In emulation of the annual U.S. State Department report on human rights violations around the world, the Hindu American Foundation (HAF), "a human rights group whose purpose," its web site [www.HinduAmericanFoundation.org] states, "is to provide a voice for the 2 million Hindu Americans in the United States," now issues an annual survey of the human rights of "Hindus in South Asia and the Diaspora." The Hindu American Foundation has appeared as Amici Curiae [friend of the Court] in cases where it feels that the state must be reminded of its obligation to preserve religious neutrality, such as in the celebrated case on whether a plaque with the Ten Commandments could be placed in a public space. HAF clearly is attuned to modern political practices: on General Pervez Musharraf's visit to the U.S. in 2006, it issued a press release on September 26th stating that the Musharraf regime had done nothing to put an end to "forced religious conversions, temple destructions and intimidation of Hindus" in Pakistan. Some of HAF's other activities point to more alarming trends, in particular strong advocacy by Hindu Americans for growing ties between India, Israel, and the United States to create an axis of countries that have, so to speak, experienced the violent fanaticism of Islam. On June 16, 2005, HAF and the American Jewish Committee jointly sponsored a program at Stanford entitled "Countering Biases Against Hindus and Jews on the College Campus." Though the program was cast in the pious languages of multiculturalism and religious pluralism, the backdrop of growing military ties, political collaboration, and intelligence sharing between India and Israel, as well as India and the U.S., is all too self-evident. Such ties have been sealed by many recent remarkable agreements, such as the American administration's decision in 2003 to allow Israel to sell its advanced Phalcon airborne reconnaissance system to India.

The spectrum of political activity is wide indeed, and agreements at the national level, such as the civilian nuclear deal—supported by the House India Caucus, led by Representative Frank Pallone (D-New Jersey), and an array of Indian American organizations including the U.S.–India Political Action Committee—between India and the U.S. in 2006, which has also been viewed with considerable euphoria by Indian Americans as a sign of their growing prowess, have hogged the limelight. It is at the local level, however, that Indian community activists and organizations have done some of their most intense lobbying, though they have not been uniformly successful. The Little India Chamber of Commerce, which represents the interests of Indian merchants who own Indian shops and restaurants across several blocks in Artesia in the metropolitan Los Angeles area, has in vain sought for over a decade to persuade the municipality to put up signs guiding visitors to "Little India." If there can be a Little Armenia, Little Thailand, Little Ethiopia, then why not a Little India?

Allegations have surfaced that Indian shopkeepers, in keeping their stores open on July 4th, have ruffled feathers; on the other hand, it is argued that unjustified stereotypes about Indians as penny-pinchers abound and even influence policymakers and politicians. Indians—and apparently others—are not likely to forget the accent-laden Apu, an Indian convenience store owner who is one of the characters in *The Simpsons*, an immensely popular television program. In one episode, Appu informs a customer, "I'll sell you expired baby food for a nickel off."

In what is perhaps its most frequent form, lobbying constitutes attempts to have "great" Indians memorialized by way of naming streets after them or having their statues installed at prominent public places. Indian communities have lobbied to place public statues of Mohandas Gandhi in numerous cities, among them Atlanta, New York, St. Louis, San Francisco, Salt Lake City, Denver, Riverside (California), and Washington, DC. Gandhi, as I have suggested in a previous chapter, is one person whose name is calculated to earn Indian Americans cultural capital, even though in private many of them are inclined to the view that the saintly old man is entirely irrelevant to a world of global capital. Gandhi even allows Indian Americans to put a different spin on Indian religions and on Hinduism as the quintessential religion of non-violence, inner harmony, and tolerance. When the Hindu American Foundation describes itself as a "non-partisan organization, promoting the Hindu and American ideals of understanding, tolerance and pluralism," it is drawing not only on the old conceit that Hinduism has uniquely among world religions stood for tolerance and religious pluralism but also on the huge reservoir of goodwill created by Gandhi.

For all their political successes and efforts, and considering the relatively high profile of the community as members of the medical, scientific, engineering, and business professions, Indian Americans nonetheless occupy a marginal place in American political life. Some members of the community see in the election of Bobby Jindal in 2004 to the U.S. House of Representatives a great ray of hope. Jindal is only the second Indian American to ever have had a seat in Congress, and his supporters have sought to minimize the fact that as an ultra-conservative Republican he embraces positions with which the Indian American community, which by a not insubstantial margin votes for Democratic candidates, is generally not in agreement. If Jindal's election points to new political possibilities for Indian Americans, the closely fought race for the governorship of Louisiana that Jindal lost equally points to the hurdles that a community which is somewhat shrouded in obscurity faces as it seeks greater political recognition. Jindal has, moreover, never expressed much interest in South Asian affairs, and he has never promoted himself as anything other than a proponent of staunchly Christian, conservative, and free market values.

Certainly no Asian Indian liberal or critic of establishment politics has exercised the kind of nearly incalculable influence on American public policy wielded by someone such as Dinesh D'Souza, who has succeeded remarkably well in presenting Asians (including Indians) as "model minorities" for African-Americans (in particular) to emulate, besides caricaturing the African-American underclass as a violent, crime-ridden, and unproductive people. It is not altogether surprising that Indian American conservatives should have risen to such public prominence: not only are their views in consonance with those of the ruling elites, but their professional status, and a narrow conception of a meritocratic society, have largely prevented them from entertaining thoughts about coalitions with Hispanics, African-Americans, and other working-class minorities. There is also more than a grain of truth in W.E.B. DuBois's observation, in 1938, that "India has also had temptation to stand apart from the darker peoples and seek her affinities among whites. She has long wished to regard herself as 'Aryan,' rather than 'colored' and to think of herself as much nearer physically and spiritually to Germany and England than to Africa, China or the South Seas. And yet, the history of the modern world shows the futility of this thought. European exploitation desires the black slave, the Chinese coolies and the Indian laborer for the same ends and the same purposes, and calls them all niggers."

As one considers the gamut of Indian political activity in the United States, there is nonetheless reason to be hopeful as well. Asian Indians have partaken of the various movements which offer a firm affirmation of the rights of cultural, religious, and ethnic minorities. Others voices have been raised in a principled critique of American domination and aggression, and a new generation of Indian Americans is contributing to more activist and progressively inclined journals such as *Colorlines*, *The Nation*, *Amerasia Journal*, and *In These Times*. Alongside the more conventional newspapers and glossy magazines, there are comparatively liberal periodicals such as *Samar* and *Little India*. While organizations such as the Network of Indian Professionals (NET-IP) and The Indus Entrepreneurs (TiE) have garnered more attention among Indian Americans, it is encouraging to think that South Asian activists have achieved resounding successes with working class populations. The work of Bhairavi Desai, Biju Mathew, and others in the New York Taxi Workers Alliance, itself an outgrowth of the Lease Drivers Coalition (LDC), formed in 1992 to represent Indian, Bangladeshi, and Pakistani cabdrivers in New York City, shows the way forward for all South Asian activists and labor union organizers. As detailed in Mathew's recent study of the taxicab business in New York City and the lives of drivers from South Asia, a large strike in 1993 was followed by a city-wide cabdrivers strike in 1998 which ground the city's cab services to a halt and offered a visceral demonstration of South Asian working class people's ability to organize across religious and ethnic lines. There is some reason, then, to believe that the multiple legacies of the Ghadr movement, the struggle for Indian independence, and the civil rights, women's, and anti-racism movements in the United States will stir Indian Americans to a greater awareness of how they may forge, for themselves and everyone else, a more just and equitable place in American society.

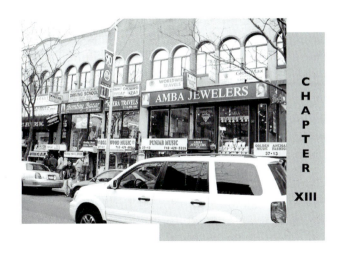

The Diaspora at Home:
Returnees, Retirees, & Resident Non-Indians

The last ten years have opened up entirely new chapters in the history of the Indian diaspora in the United States. We need a language that would encompass several categories of Indians who have been overlooked, even in recent histories of the Indian diasporas, and whose experiences reasonably stretch the perhaps already overextended reach of the word "diaspora." Who would have thought, even five years ago, that 30,000 Americans and Britishers would be working today in the information technology industries in India? Their history, admittedly, cannot easily be woven into the history of the Indian diaspora, even if that history is partly a consequence of the emergence of an Indian diaspora in the United States. For four decades, one has been hearing of the graduates of leading Indian universities who made their way to the United States, and though it would be premature to speak at this juncture of a brain drain from the United States, an accelerating reverse flow now seems all but certain. If the Indians who, especially in recent years, have started trickling back to India demand some attention, there is also the perplexing question of how we are to accommodate those left behind, particularly the often retired parents of single children. Beyond all this, there is the question of the some 200 million Indians who the sociologist D.L. Sheth once trenchantly if humorously characterized as the Resident Non-Indians. These are the middle-class Indians who have never left India, of if they have, they have gone no farther than Dubai or Singapore. They have set their sights on America, on the elusive greencard; in their mind, they already live in America, even if they do not own a slice of it.

Let me begin first with the returnees, since they constitute the smallest of these groups that comprise what I would like to call the liminal history of the Indian diaspora. No exact figures are available, but it is estimated that in 2005 there may have been some 15,000 Indian American professionals who took up job offers in India. The *New York Times*, in an article on December 26, 2005, cited an estimate from Nasscom, a group representing Indian outsourcing companies, of about 30,000 professionals of Indian origin who had returned to India in the previous eighteen months. The number of Indian Americans voyaging back to the eternal motherland has been accelerating in recent years, and the trend first commenced in significant numbers around 2,000, some ten years after reforms to "jump start" the flailing Indian economy were first launched. It is reasonable to aver that only a small percentage of the returnees of the last few years will give up their American citizenship or permanent residency at this juncture, and it is just as reasonable to suppose that a significant percentage of the Returned Non-Resident Indians (RNRI), if this neologism may be permitted, will eventually make their way back to the United States and so join the ranks of what I would term the Twice Returned Non-Resident Indian (TRNRI). The anecdotal evidence for the return migration to India is certainly strong, even if desperate researchers have not sprung at the opportunity to string together previously uncollected data, and doubtless the conditions for a return are quite propitious. Though farmers in several Indian states have in alarming numbers, as many as 50,000 of them, committed suicide over the last decade, certain segments of the Indian economy are booming. There are vast fortunes to be made, not only inherited, in India today, a point underscored in *Time Asia*'s clichéd cover story of January 2005, "A Tale of Two Indias." Or, to cite a report that has initiated a fever of excitement in India, *Forbes* reported, in its story on "The World's Richest People" on 8 March 2007, that "after a 20-year reign, Japan is no longer Asia's top spot for billionaires: India has 36, worth a total of $191 billion, followed by Japan with 24, worth a combined $64 billion." The returnees who work in information technologies, software industries, biotechnology, investment banking, venture capital, and other profitable ventures think not only of the frenetic pace with which India is being transformed and of millionaires being created overnight, but of the comforts, not to be gained at any but the most exorbitant price in the U.S., of a labor-intensive Indian society.

Many Indian Americans always had, as I have previously suggested, lingering doubts about "American culture" and the moral risks of raising children in American society. Not long ago they dared only to voice their doubts and resentments at dinner parties among fellow Indians, but the prospects of return were never imminent: not only were the attractions of the dollar much too strong and the job prospects in India poor, but they feared that their children would find India, with its pollution, electricity breakdowns, water shortages, dense crowds, filth and poverty, difficult if not intolerable. But the rapid transformation of Indian cities, to which Indian Americans who have visited in recent years attest with evident pride, has now given rise to new possibilities. If an American Eden can be created in India, and the work habits, canons of good management, the ethos of efficiency, the horizontal and vertical grids of American cities, and the squeaky cleanliness of Protestant America can be introduced into India without the equally numerous hazards of the land of freedom, from schools with pathetic academic standards and widespread acceptance of sexual promiscuity to the vacuousness of youth culture and the lack of authentic cultural traditions, then why not settle in India? These returned NRIs move into American-style enclaves and gated communities with names like Green Meadows, Hanging Gardens, Lake View, Emerald Isle, Bel-Air

Estates, and Regent's Park. They command, in some cases, American salaries, certainly incomes that allow them to lead exceedingly comfortable lives in India. Very little of India is allowed to intrude into their world of carefully manicured and watered lawns, swimming pools, backyards with barbecues, and something truly calculated to make Indians stop, namely intersections with STOP signs. The returnees seek to bring to India what they consider a more evolved American sensitivity to the needs of working mothers, the physically challenged, children with learning disabilities, and the like. I am reminded of Indian American friends raising a young daughter in a major American city who suffers from a life-threatening peanut allergy. The entire school that she attends has been declared a peanut-free zone, and though the returnees may not be necessarily inclined to pursue the same ends in an Indian city, they would point to such care and sensitivity as an instantiation of America's unique regard for the rights of the individual.

For all their love of the motherland, their desire to give back something to the country where they most likely earned their first degrees at the government's expense, and their happiness at seeing their children grow and learn in close proximity to grandparents, the returnees remain persuaded that in most social mores, and in its treatment of minorities, the United States is leap years ahead of India. The returnees, however, are also an avidly consuming class, and they set standards of emulation for Indians outside their gated communities. Their swimming pools, water around the clock, assured electricity supply, and SUVs are an enormous drain on already scarce resources. They may not come back to India as a colonizing class, but their attempt to recreate in Bangalore or Hyderabad the America they have left behind is more than faintly reminiscent of the ethos of the British colonizers who sought to render India familiar through institutions, such as private clubs and hill stations, which evoked particular conceptions of Englishness. Back home in Britain after a decade or two in India, the "nabobs" were envied, despised, and ridiculed not only because they had accumulated vast fortunes and so poked a hole in the lifestyles of the landed aristocracy, but because their wealth put them in a position of being able to influence the course of politics. Much the same questions, sooner rather than later, will have to be asked of the returnees.

Among the returnees, some doubtless have had much occasion to think of their parents who were left behind. It is not uncommon to find parents of Indian Americans, especially those who in turn are young parents, visiting their children and grandchildren for periods of as long as six months. But for as many retired people who spend a good portion of the year with their children in the U.S., there are as many who refuse to be lured by the attractions of a comfortable life in an American suburb. Some are understandably reluctant to forgo the social networks and the familiarity of social mores and everyday interactions nurtured over a lifetime for an uncertain future with their children in the U.S. Others fear that they might become a burden on their children, or that they might make themselves vulnerable to their children and become something like second-class citizens in the homes of their sons (and daughters). Among elderly parents who have visited their children in the U.S., many have been heard saying that the U.S. is akin to a "prison." This assessment comes not from an awareness that the United States perhaps holds the largest prison population in the world, or that the construction and management of prisons is one of the most profitable private enterprises, but from the overwhelming experience of confinement many of them experience in suburban neighborhoods without public transportation systems. In a land preeminently associated with the cult of mobility, they ironically find themselves immobile, wholly dependent on the goodwill of their grown-up children to ferry them to the supermarket or nearest temple, mosque, or gurdwara.

Increasingly, thus, the loneliness and plight of the retirees is becoming a feature of the social landscape of Indian urban life. If social histories of war are attentive to the families of soldiers who await the return of their menfolk (and, in some cases, womenfolk) from the battlefield, we must ask why social histories of diasporas have paid so little attention to the families of immigrants. The post-1965 middle-class and, in most instances, highly educated immigrants also belonged to the generation among whom the size of families had shrunk, and though the Indian immigrant was not often the only child, he seldom had more than one or two siblings and almost always he left behind in India parents who were at least in their late forties and often in their fifties or older. In India, the retirement age until recently has been fifty-eight for salaried employees of central, state, and local governments, and even in corporations and private businesses seldom extended to beyond sixty. The parents who were left behind thus had, in many instances, ceased to have an active work life. Over the last decade, certainly, the phenomenon of elderly parents now fending for themselves, receiving an occasional visit from a son settled in the U.S., or a married daughter now relocated to another urban center, has become much more widespread.

The Hindi feature film *Dattak*, though far from being a cinematic masterpiece, has nicely captured some of the problems that have arisen in recent years. A son returns to India from the United States in search of his aged father, whom he has not seen for fifteen years, only to find the house locked and his father untraceable. His own siblings, scattered across different parts of the country, have no knowledge of the whereabouts of their father. Slowly, through persistent queries, he becomes aware of the kindness showered upon his father by a stranger, and the dire straits to which his father is reduced when, at the sudden death of this stranger, he finds himself without the solace of friends or family. The son's search leads him to a retirement home, only to find that his father had passed away. In his quest to discover how his father lived the last few months of his life, the son befriends another old resident of the retirement home; finally, in what is not only a supreme act of atonement, but a gesture that humanity does not stop at the borders of blood, he seeks the old man's permission to "adopt" him as his father. The old man finally finds a son; the son, at long last, enters into a relationship with a man whom he can accept as a father. The film by no means descends to a trite and unreflective critique of the Non-resident Indian as a heartless, narcissistic creature interested only in his own advancement; indeed, in his treatment of the subject, the director is if anything more harsh towards the protagonist's siblings, who while remaining within India display supreme indifferent to their father, and he is critical of the urban culture of modern India which no longer recognizes traditional moral obligations.

The Non-resident Indian, such as the protagonist of *Dattak*, may still retain something of a hankering for the imagined social bonds of a lifestyle that was abandoned for the creature comforts of life in the fast lane. The urban Indian in Mumbai, Delhi, or Bangalore, it is possible to argue, has no such illusions—or such illusions persist only among those who have recently come into the city from the countryside, and who amidst the harshness, anomie, and competitiveness of urban existence initially yearn for the simplicity of village life. Theorists of the diaspora have for some years been disputing whether the notion of the diaspora necessarily entails the idea of an eventual return to the homeland, or whether such a conception of the diaspora is too strongly hitched to histories of the Jewish diaspora. And yet all such accounts of the diaspora, however divergent their conclusions, are still rooted in a diaspora which has taken shape in a positivistic geography. Some in the diaspora eventually make their peace with the motherland; but, it is my submission, a different restlessness characterizes the lives of those who, without ever having left India, already imagine themselves as part of the fabric of American life.

The phenomenon of the Resident Non-Indian has numerous manifestations, extending from the widespread indulgence in American pop culture and the fiction of Robert Ludlum and Stephen King to the fervor with which metropolitan Indians have embraced American mall culture, slang, and mores of intimacy. Over several years in the recent past disputes, sometimes turning violent, have broken out over the celebration by young people of Valentine's Day and the stated ambition of Hindu extremists to thwart such festivities on the grounds that open displays of romantic (and sexual) love represent the ascendancy of a shameless American culture and are violative of the social norms of Indian society. Such disputes appear to pit the traditionalists versus the modernists, nationalists versus internationalists, prudes versus liberals, the upholders of a parochial conception of culture against multiculturalists and proponents of globalization. If the Hindu militants appear in this conflict to be pathetically bereft of any confidence in the capaciousness of a civilization that has weathered many a more virulent storm, the advocates of Valentine's Day seem wholly unaware that Valentine's Day, far from being a spontaneous celebration of the joyousness of romantic love, is one of those many regimented exercises in mindless consumption which owes its origins largely to the marketing ingenuity of Hallmark Cards. What Indians who seek to enshrine Valentine's Day as a universal holiday are embracing is not a romantic conception of love, or even the notion of individual choice or freedom of lifestyles, but rather, even if unwittingly, an American conception of the market which has drawn toothpaste, deodorants, Valentine's Day Cards, roses, chocolates, sexy lingerie, and much else into the same orbit of romantic love.

The various ways in which the diaspora comes home to roost was never brought home to me with greater clarity than one November evening about ten years ago when I chanced upon a large sign outside the Priya cinema hall, frequented mostly by highly Westernized Indians in the affluent neighborhood of Vasant Vihar in South Delhi, advertising "Thanksgiving Turkeys." The history of the Pilgrims, much less that of American Indians—still characterized, if innocently, by an older generation of Indians as "Red Indians"—is not part of the repertoire of educated Indians, and the turkey has no place in Indian folklore or mythology—or, for that matter, on Indian dinner tables. We may say that the Indian consumers of "Thanksgiving Turkeys" in one of Delhi's wealthier neighborhoods left India long ago; with full body and soul, they imagine themselves as belonging to America. They have some encouragement in thinking so from the brute realities of Indian migration to the United States. It seems, from everyday conversation, that nearly every middle-class family, not only in Delhi, Bangalore, Mumbai, Ahmedabad, and Kolkata, but even in the comparatively smaller cities of Jaipur, Lucknow,

Ludhiana, and Jullunder, now has at least one member residing in the United States. There is a much wider Indian diaspora beyond the United States, and the term Non-resident Indian in principle extends to all diasporic Indians, but it has always been understood that the diasporic Indian who one might envy was the one who had gone to America. Twenty years ago, matrimonial ads for grooms and brides alike in the Sunday newspapers began to feature a special category entitled "Green Card Holder." Truly has the Indian diaspora in America spawned in India its own history. Any future history of the Indian diaspora in the United States will thus have to take stock not only of the green card holders, but of those whose whole lives are dedicated to obtaining one, those who have become Resident Non-Indians. Goodbye, Non-resident Indians, the future may lie elsewhere.

SOURCES AND SELECT FURTHER READING

Note: Books, articles, and other sources (including websites) mentioned in the body of the paper are generally not mentioned here. This is intended to be a selective guide to the literature.

Chapter I: Indians in the Global Setting

Brij V. Lal, Peter Reeves, and Rajesh Rai, eds., *The Encyclopedia of the Indian Diaspora* (Singapore: Editions Didier Millet with the National University of Singapore, 2006), which was released just as the first draft of this book was being completed, furnishes the most complete overview of the Indian diaspora. *South Asians Overseas: Migration and Ethnicity*, eds. Colin Clarke, Ceri Peach and Steven Vertovec (Cambridge: Cambridge University Press, 1990), is the best scholarly anthology on the subject, though there are more specialized anthologies, such as Peter van der Veer, ed., *Nation and Migration: The Politics of Space in the South Asian Diaspora* (Philadelphia: University of Pennsylvania Press, 1995). The rather tenuous place of diasporic Indians is discussed by Vinay Lal, "Labor and Longing: The Rights of Indians in the Diaspora," *Seminar* 538 (June 2004): 14–26.

Comprehensive histories of immigrants in the United States until comparatively recently devoted very little space to Indian immigrants, though with the burgeoning Indian population this is no longer the case. South Asian Americans traditionally occupied an ambivalent position in narrative histories of Asian Americans, which were generally focused on East Asians, but more recent histories of Asian Americans have doubtless been more accommodating to South Asians, which is scarcely surprising considering that immigrants from India have been outpacing all other immigrants barring the Mexicans. Jean Yu-wen Shen Wu and Min Sung's edited reader, *Asian American Studies* (New Brunswick: Rutgers University Press, 2000), provides perhaps the best introduction to the field of Asian American Studies. Ronald Takaki has been among those scholars of Asian American Studies who has always been attentive to South Asians: see *Strangers from a Different Shore: A History of Asian Americans* (New York: Penguin, 1989). Joel Kotkin, *Tribes: How Race, Religion and Identity Determine Success in the New Global Economy* (New York: Random House, 1993), offers a short readable account of "The Greater India."

The global context of indentured labor in the nineteenth century is captured in David Northrup, *Indentured Labor in the Age of Imperialism, 1834–1922* (Cambridge: Cambridge University Press, 1995). However, for sheer intellectual perspicacity, conjoined to an ethical perspective, it would be difficult to match Marina Carter and Khal Torabully, *Coolitude: An Anthology of the Indian Labour Diaspora* (London: Anthem, 2002).

There are fewer comprehensive histories of Indian Americans than one might imagine. Roger Daniels, *History of Indian Immigration to the United States: An Interpretive Essay* (New York: The Asia Society, 1989), is short and sweet; more incisive, politically daring, and combative is Vijay Prashad, *The Karma of Brown Folk* (Minneapolis: University of Minnesota Press, 2000). Karen Isaksen Leonard, *The South Asian Americans* (Westport: Greenwood Press, 1997), makes an attempt to be wide-ranging but could have been more analytical.

Darshan Singh Tatla, *The Sikh Diaspora: The Search for Statehood* (London: University College London Press, 1999), is similarly a global history of the Sikh diaspora though the accent is on the political history of Sikh diasporic communities in the United States and United Kingdom.

There are more recent impressionistic accounts where the Indian diaspora can be seen through its fragments. The more arresting of these narratives include Jael Silliman, *Jewish Portraits, Indian Frames: Women's Narratives from a Diaspora of Hope* (Calcutta: Seagull Books, 2001 and Hanover: University Press of New England, 2003); Mira Kamdar, *Motiba's Tattoos: A Granddaughter's Journey from America Into Her Indian Family's Past* (New York: Plume Books, 2001); and, especially, Amitava Kumar, *Passport Photos* (Berkeley: University of California Press, 2000), as well as *Bombay London New York* (London: Routledge, 2002).

Chapter II: Passage to India: The Circulation of the Orient in Americas

The circulation of "India" from the eighteenth to the early nineteenth century in New England can be gleaned from James Duncan Phillips, *Salem and the Indies* (Boston: Houghton Mifflin, 1947); Gauri Viswanathan, "Yale College and the Culture of British Imperialism", *Yale Journal of Criticism* 7:1 (1994): 1–30; and Gavin Weightman, *The Frozen-Water Trade* (New York: Hyperion, 2003).

There is a prolific literature on the presence of Indian thought in the writings of Emerson and Thoreau: see Vinay Lal, *Emerson and*

India (unpublished M.A. thesis, Johns Hopkins University, 1982); Arthur Versluis, *American Transcendentalism and Asian Religions* (New York: Oxford University Press, 1993); and Alan Hodder, "Ex Oriente Lux: Thoreau's Ecstasies and the Hindu Texts," *Harvard Theological Review* 86:4 (1994). Older studies, such as those of Frederic Ives Carpenter, *Emerson and Asia* (Cambridge, Mass: Harvard University Press, 1930), and Arthur E. Christy, *The Orient in American Transcendentalism* (New York: Columbia University Press, 1932), though there are several more, are severely compromised by their Orientalist outlook and are even otherwise dated. Among primary texts, Thoreau's *A Week on the Concord and Merrimack Rivers* (various editions) is much lesser known than *Walden*, though the Tuesday chapter offers a clear insight into Thoreau's regard for early Indian philosophical literature. Emerson's short poem, "Brahma", has been widely anthologized.

The Grand Canyon and Las Vegas as two unexpected sites of Hinduism are explored in Vinay Lal, "Ambiences of Hinduism in the Wild West of America", *Suitcase* 2:1–2 (1997): 84–97.

Chapter III: Voyage from India: Slaves and Seamen, Workers and Peasants
     California and the Oriental: *Japanese, Chinese, and Hindus*, which is the report of the State Board of Control of California (1920), represents the official view at a time when restrictions on Asian immigration into the U.S. had already come into place (reprint ed., New York: Arno Press, 1978). Sucheta Mazumdar furnishes a Marxist perspective on Indian labor in the Punjab and on the West Coast in "Colonial Impact and Punjabi Emigration to the United States" and "Punjabi Agricultural Workers in California, 1905-1945", both in Lucie Cheng and Edna Bonacich, eds., *Labor Immigration under Capitalism*: *Asian Workers in the United States before World War II* (Berkeley: University of California Press, 1984). Much less exciting, though broader in scope, is Bruce La Brack, *The Sikhs of Northern California, 1904-1975*: *A Socio-Historical Study* (New York: AMS Press, 1988).

Chapter IV: The Diaspora within the Diaspora: Students and Rebels
     The early political history of Indian Americans has attracted a wide body of scholarly and popular work. The best known of these studies is Joan M. Jensen, *Passage from India*: *Asian Indian Immigrants in North America* (New Haven: Yale University Press, 1988). A substantial mythography has developed around the short-lived Ghadr

movement, with well over a dozen full-length studies. The Government of India's account of revolutionary unrest on the west coast is to be found in James Campbell Ker, *Political Trouble in India, 1907–1917* (Calcutta: Superintendent, Government Printing, 1917; reprint, Delhi: Oriental Publishers, 1973). T.R. Sareen, *Indian Revolutionary Movement Abroad, 1905–1921* (New Delhi: Sterling Publishers, 1979), and Sohan Singh Josh, *Hindustan Gadar Party: A Short History*, 2 vols. (New Delhi: People's Publishing House, 1977–1978), are reliable. Mark Juergensmeyer's much-circulated article on the "Gadar syndrome" is collected together in a useful anthology which remains indispensable for the study of early Indian immigration to the U.S.: see C. Chandrasekhar, ed., *From India to America: A Brief History of Immigration; Problems of Discrimination; Admission and Assimilation* (La Jolla: Population Review Books, 1982). Rajani Kanta Das was not only a witness to the events, but wrote from the standpoint of labor: see his *Hindustani Workers on the Pacific Coast* (Berlin: Walter de Gruyter & Co., 1923).

Harold A. Gould, Sikhs, *Swamis, Students and Spies: The India Lobby in the United States, 1900-1946* (New Delhi: Sage Publishers, 2006), comes highly recommended though it came to my attention after this and the preceding chapter had been completed. Some of the more important writings of the Indian intellectuals discussed in this chapter are enumerated in the body of the text.

Chapter V: "Tawnies" Amidst Whites (after Benjamin Franklin)

The Library of America volume on Benjamin Franklin (New York, 1987) has been used for Benjamin Franklin's essay, "Observations Concerning the Increase of Mankind."

Sucheta Mazumdar, "Racist Responses to Racism: The Aryan Myth and South Asians in the United States", *South Asia Bulletin* 9:1 (1989): 47-55 was a foundational piece. Intimate relations between Asians and whites, fraught with danger, are discussed in Susan Koshy, *Sexual Naturalization: Asian Americans and Miscegenation* (Stanford: Stanford University Press, 2004).

The legal history of discrimination against Asians Americans, including those from South Asia, has been recounted in numerous texts. Bill Ong Hing, *Making and Remaking Asian America Through Immigration Policy, 1850-1990* (Stanford: Stanford University Press, 1993), is comprehensive and authoritative. With particular reference to South Asians, the essays collected together in the aforementioned S. Chandrasekhar, *From India to America* (La Jolla, California: Population Review Book, 1982), are of much use. The incident of the steamship Komagata Maru has been the subject of a recent feature-length documentary by Ali Kazimi, "Continuous Journey" (2004). The official narrative is best encountered through *Report of the Komagata Maru Committee of Inquiry* (Calcutta: Government Printing, Government of India, 1914), while the best scholarly account is Hugh Johnston, *Voyage of the Komagata Maru: The Sikh Challenge to Canada's Colour Bar* (Delhi: Oxford University Press, 1979).

Chapter VI: Exile in the New Canaan

Karen Isaksen Leonard has written the most widely read study of California's Punjabi Mexican Americans, *Making Ethnic Choices* (Philadelphia: Temple University Press, 1994). Two primary texts come readily to mind from the period between the 1920s and the passage of the 1965 INS Act: Dhan Gopal Mukerji, *Caste and Outcaste* (1923; new ed. with introduction by Akhil Gupta and Purnima Mankekar (Stanford: Stanford University Press, 2000), and Dalip Singh Saund, *Congressman from India* (New York: E. P. Dutton, 1960).

Octavio Paz served a short stint in India in the late 1950s before returning to India as Mexico's ambassador, a position he held from 1962 until his resignation in 1968 in protest against the violent repression of student unrest in Mexico. Paz was prolific in the expression of his views on Indian history, culture, and politics, with which he would have a profound engagement for the rest of his life. A collection of his essays, *In Light of India*, translated by Eliot Weinberger (New York: Harcourt, 1997), serves as the best introduction to his writings on India.

Though a resolutely intellectual and thorough account of African American appropriations of Gandhi's strategies of mass nonviolent resistance, and a more general history of African American views of Indian nationalism within which Gandhi is embedded is still awaited, an adequate beginning has been made by Sudarshan Kapur, *Raising Up a Prophet: The African-American Encounter with Gandhi* (Boston: Beacon Press, 1992).

Chapter VII: Emergence of a Diasporic Community

The Indian community in the post-1965 period, and more particularly since a considerable presence first became established in the 1980s, has been the subject of numerous monographic studies and edited volumes. Among them are Maxine P. Fisher, *The Indians of New York City* (New Delhi: Heritage Publishers, 1980); A. Wesley Helweg and Usha M. Helweg, *An Immigrant Success Story: East Indians in America* (Philadelphia: University of Pennsylvania Press, 1990); Padma Rangaswamy, *Namaste America: Indian Immigrants in an American Metropolis* (University Park: Pennsylvania State University Press, 2000); Bandana Purkayastha, *Negotiating Ethnicity: Second-Generation South Asian Americans Traverse a Transnational World* (New Brunswick: Rutgers University Press, 2005); Sandhya Shukla, *India Abroad: Diasporic Cultures of Postwar America and England* (Princeton: Princeton University Press, 2003); and a volume edited by Lavina Shankar and Rajini Srikanth, *A Part, Yet Apart: South Asians in Asian America* (Philadelphia: Temple University Press, 1988).

A more glossy literature on the accomplishments of Indians is also emerging. As an example of something in the celebratory mode, see Gurmukh Singh, *California Dreams: India Shining in the Land of Hollywood* (Vancouver: British Columbia Books Publication, 2006), which profiles successful Indian Californians. (What constitutes "success" is, of course, never put into question.) A second-generation voice, more attuned to the politics of multiculturalism and somewhat less enamored of the American dream, is best encountered in S. Mitra Kalita, *Suburban Sahibs: Three Immigrant Families and Their Passage from India to America* (New Brunswick: Rutgers University Press, 2003).

The so-called "brain drain" from India has been investigated at great length by Binod Khadria. Much of his work is available in the form of specialized papers and monographs written for international agencies such as the International Labour Office (ILO, Geneva) and Organisation for Economic Cooperation and Development (OECD, in Paris). His important studies include *Migration of Highly Skilled Indians: Case Studies of IT and Health Professionals* (OECD, 2004); *Human Resources in Science and Technology in India and the International Mobility of Highly Skilled Indians* (OECD, 2004); and *Skilled Labour Migration from Developing Countries, Study on India* (ILO, 2002). More accessible are *Migration of Knowledge Workers, Second-Generation Effects of India's Brain Drain* (New Delhi: Sage Publications, 1999) and "Of Dreams, Drain, and Dams—Metaphors in the Indian Emigration of Talent", *India International Centre Quarterly* 26:3 (Monsoon 1999): 79–90. An economic, demographic, and comparative portrait of Silicon Valley's Indians is available in AnnaLee Saxenian, *Silicon Valley's New Immigrant Entrepreneurs* (San Diego: Center for Comparative Immigration Studies at University of California, 2000), but shockingly little has been written of the social and cultural lives of these fabled seekers of dreams and fortunes.

Chapter VIII: The Religious Life of Indian Communities

Raymond Brady Williams has devoted the better part of his scholarly life to the study of the transmission of the religious traditions of South Asia to the West. His edited volume, *A Sacred Thread*: *Modern Transmission of Hindu Traditions in India and Abroad* (New York: Columbia University Press, 1996 [1992]) is a good starting point. His earlier study, *Religions of Immigrants from India and Pakistan*: *New Threads in the American Tapestry* (Cambridge: Cambridge University Press, 1988), has a broader canvas; conversely, *An Introduction to Swaminarayan Hinduism* (Cambridge: Cambridge University Press, 2001), moves in the opposite direction and focuses on a sectarian tradition of Hinduism which, especially in its diasporic setting, has come to considerable prominence in recent years. *Christian Pluralism in the United States*: *The Indian Immigrant Experience* (Cambridge: Cambridge University Press, 1996), focuses on the small number of Indian American Christians, though its case for the importance of Indian Christianity in altering the fabric of American Christian life is not wholly persuasive. The diverse strands of Raymond Williams's writings on South Asian religions in the worldwide Indian diaspora are represented in *Williams on South Asian Religions and Immigration* (Aldershot, Hampshire: Ashgate, 2004).

Vivekananda's travels and speaking tours in the United States are marvelously captured in Marie Louise Burke, *Swami Vivekananda in America*, *New Discoveries* (San Francisco: Vedanta Society, 1958; 2nd rev. ed., Calcutta: Advaita Ashram, 1966). Wendell Thomas, *Hinduism Invades America* (New York: Beacon Press, 1930), is much less alarmist than the title suggests; quite to the contrary, it displays a certain prescience in its suggestion that Eastern religions, here encapsulated under the rubric of "Hinduism", would find many seekers in the United States.

Diana L. Eck, most well-known to scholars of Hinduism and Indic studies for her elegant study of Benares, has lately been involved in comprehending the diversity of religious experience in the United

States. Though Islam in the United States is understood by most Americans to be a religion predominantly of the Middle East, South Asia is, in actuality, home to more Muslims than any other part of the world. Indian Muslims, Buddhists, and Sikhs play a part in Eck's recent study, *A New Religious America*: *How a 'Christian Country' Has Become the World's Most Religiously Diverse Nation* (New York: Harper-Collins, 2001), though the predominantly Hindu community receives the most extended treatment.

Chapter IX: Indian "Culture" in the Diaspora

Recent scholarly work has drawn attention to previously neglected constituencies in the Indian population. Sunaina Maira, *Desis in the House: Indian American Youth Culture in New York City* (Philadelphia: Temple University Press, 2002), and Rakesh Ratti, ed., *A Lotus of Another Color*: *An Unfolding of the South Asian Gay and Lesbian Experience* (Boston: Alyson Publications, 1993), are the most prominent illustrations of this type of literature. In general, however, the scholarly attention that bhangra and South Asian dance music in Britain have attracted remains unique. Nearly every "cultural studies" work on Indians in Britain has felt bound to explore the lyrics of Apache Indian.

There are no monograph-length works on the various cultural formations, discussed in this chapter, that the Indian diaspora in the U.S. has taken. It is remarkable to what extent local Indian communities are immersed in the culture of the spelling bee, but more insights into this are to be found in the film *Spellbound* (2002, director: Jeffrey Blitz) than in any literature. Though it is a documentary, viewers found it entrancing, even suspenseful, and the film had, considering the subject matter, an extraordinarily successful run. On the equally ubiquitous presence of Bharatnatyam in middle-class and professional South Asian families with daughters, see Anita Kumar, "What's the Matter? Shakti's (Re)Collection of Race, Nationhood, and Gender", *The Drama Review* 50, no. 4 (Winter 2006): 72-94.

The Hindu Students Council and VHP-America are best explored in periodical literature. A good beginning is Biju Mathew, "Byte-Sized Nationalism: Mapping the Hindu Right in the United States", *Rethinking Marxism* 12:3 (Fall 2000): 108-128; much less analytical is Jawaid Quddus, "Hindutva and Indian Diaspora," in Ram Puniyani, ed., *Religion, Power and Violence*: *Expression of Politics in Contemporary Times*

(New Delhi: Sage Publications, 2005). Prema Kurien has discussed the Hindu Student Council and other manifestations of Hindu youth culture in "Being Young, Brown, and Hindu: The Identity Struggles of Second-Generation Indian Americans," *Journal of Contemporary Ethnography* 34:4 (August 2005): 434–469.

Chapter X: The Politics of Affluence and the Anxiety of Influence

Some of the arguments of this chapter have been explored at greater length by the author in "India in the World: Hinduism, the Diaspora and the Anxiety of Influence", *Australian Religion Studies Review* 16:2 (Spring 2003): 19–37. Anecdotal and journalistic accounts of the Patels in America proliferate, but a full-length scholarly study is still awaited. Govind B. Bhakta, *Patels: A Gujarati Community History in the United States* (Los Angeles: UCLA Asian American Studies Center, 2002), is largely descriptive but nonetheless useful. The mention of Indians as motel owners in the American deep south occurs early in V.S. Naipaul's *A Turn in the South* (New York: Alfred A. Knopf, 1989).

The category of the Non-Resident Indian (NRI) is usefully explored in the annual reports of the Ministry of External Affairs, Government of India, as well as in the proceedings of the Pravasi Bharatiya Divas, though here as well a compelling scholarly study is lacking. Marie-Carine Lall, *India's Missed Opportunity: India's Relationship with the Non-Resident Indians* (Aldershot: Ashgate, 2001) is adequate though prosaic. The charitable acts of Kanwal Rekhi, Gururaj Deshpande, and others are enumerated in Priya Viswanath, *Diaspora Indians—On the Philanthropy Fast-Track* (Mumbai: Centre for the Advancement of Philanthropy, 2004). Mark Sidel, "Diaspora Philanthropy to India: A Perspective from the United States", offers the best overview of the subject. It is one of three papers on gift-giving from the Indian diaspora in Peter F. Geithner, Paula D. Johnson, and Lincoln C. Chen, eds., *Diaspora Philanthropy and Equitable Development in China and India* (Cambridge, Mass: Global Equity Initiative, Asia Center, Harvard University, 2004).

Chapter XI: The Landscapes of Representation in Internet Modernity

The literary aspects of the Indian diaspora are explored in a sophisticated recent study by Sudesh Mishra, *Diaspora Theory* (Edinburgh: Edinburgh University Press, 2006). Another theoretical treatment is R. Radhakrishnan, *Diasporic Meditations: Between Home and Location* (Minneapolis: University of Minnesota Press, 1996). There are several detailed studies of South Asian American literature; especially worthy of study is Rajini Srikanth, *The World Next Door: South Asian American Literature and the Idea of America* (Philadelphia: Temple University Press, 2004).

An account of some South Asian intellectuals in the U.S. and UK is to be found in Jackie Assayag and Veronique Benei, eds., *At Home in Diaspora: South Asian Scholars and the West* (New Delhi: Permanent Black, 2003).

"The Campaign To Stop Funding Hate" collaborated with Sabrang Communications in Mumbai, publishers of *Communalism Combat*, and The South Asia Citizens Web, an extraordinary list serve and web site initiated by Harsh Kapoor in France, to produce *The Foreign Exchange of Hate: IDRF and the American Funding of Hindutva* (2002). The report is available online [http://www.proxsa.org/newsflash/index.html]; and the intense, usually vitriolic, criticism it generated among supporters of IDRF and Hindutva is also best gauged by a survey of online responses at such forums as www.sulekha.com and www.rediff.com.

The numerous documents generated by the California Textbooks controversy have been collected at the web site of the Friends of South Asia [FOSA], an activist peace group established in 2001 [www.friendsofsouthasia.org]. FOSA maintains a special web page on the "California Textbooks Issue" [www.friendsofsouthasia.org/textbook]. Vinay Lal, "North American Hindus, the Sense of History, and the Politics of Internet Diasporism", in *Asian-America.Net: Ethnicity, Nationalism, and Cyberspace*, eds. Rachel C. Lee and Sau-ling Cynthia Wong (London & New York: Routledge, 2003): 98–138 is still the most extended treatment of the politics of the internet in Indian American communities.

Among the more assiduous chroniclers of South Asian women in the U.S. is Shamita Das Dasgupta: see the edited volume, *A Patchwork Shawl: Chronicles of South Asian Women in America* (New Brunswick: Rutgers University Press, 1998). Margaret Abraham, *Speaking the Unspeakable: Marital Violence among South Asian Immigrants in the United States* (New Brunswick: Rutgers University Press, 2000), is the best book on this subject.

Chapter XII Politics and the Future of Indians in the U.S.

Two special issues of *Amerasia Journal* delve deeply into South Asian politics in the U.S.: "Satyagraha in America: The Political Culture of South Asian Americans," Vol. 25:3 (1999/2000), guest-edited by Biju Mathew and Vijay Prashad, and "Deporting Our Souls & Defending Our Immigrants," Vol. 31:3 (2005), guest-edited by Bill Ong Hing. Biju Mathew makes a living as a professor of business at Rider University, but for ten years he rode cabs, became intimate with taxi drivers, and adopted their struggle for a decent living as his own. The results are to be seen in his riveting account, at once an ethnography of the taxi business and the lives of cabs drivers as much as a critique of globalization, called *Taxi! Cabs and Capitalism in New York City* (New York: The New Press, 2005).

The politics of Sikhism in the United States is discussed in Vinay Lal, "Sikh Kirpans in California Schools: The Social Construction of Symbols, the Cultural Politics of Identity, and the Limits of Multiculturalism," in David K. Yoo, ed., *New Spiritual Homes: Religion and Asian Americans* (Honolulu: University of Hawaii Press, 1999): 77-133.

The New York–New Jersey area is doubtless the most important site of South Asian activism. The magazine *SAMAR* [South Asian Magazine for Action and Reflection; www.samarmagazine.org] is published from there, and it is home to most members of FOIL [Forum of the Indian Left; www.foil.org].

Within the confines of this book it has not been possible to offer more than a token mention of those members of the Indian diaspora who, at present, occupy a somewhat liminal space in Indian communities. I am thinking, for example, of Indo-Trinidadians and Indo-Guyanese who are now settled, in substantial numbers, in the New York - New Jersey area. Will they be counted as Indo-Caribbean Americans, or is it likely that, like the Gujaratis who fled Uganda and Kenya, they will simply be viewed as Indian Americans or, in certain circles, as Gujarati Americans? They have been accommodated under the rubric of the Indian diaspora by such organizations as GOPIO, the Global Organization of People of Indian Origin, but both their attachment to the Caribbean and their dissociation from India prevent their easy assimilation to any preconceived notion of homeland. One of the few volumes on this growing population is Alina Camacho-Gingerich, ed., *Coping in America: The Case of Caribbean East Indians* (New York: The Guyanese East Indian Civic Association, 2002).

INDEX

A

AAHOA (see Asian American Hotel Owners Association)
Advani, Mukesh 101
Afghanistan xii, 26, 120
African Americans 33-35, 48, 54-55, 125
AHAD (see American Hindus Against Defamation)
Akshardham (BAPS) temples 71
Alexander, Meena 110-11
Ali, Agha Shahid 110
American Hindus Against Defamation 102-04
American Indians ix-x, 134
American Oriental Society 10
Americas, the ix
Anderson, Benedict 30
Apu, character in Simpsons 124
Aryan, Aryans viii, 35-38, 42, 54, 125
Asian American Hotel Owners Association 94-98
Asian Americans 15-16, 54-56
    discrimination against 15-16
Asian Indians x-xi
    brought as slaves 13-14
    (see also Indian Americans)
Asiatic Exclusion League 21-22
Association of Indians in America (AIA) 61
Association of Pakistani Professionals 120
Association of Physicians of Indian Origin (AAPI) 61-63
Atlantic Charter 50
ayurveda 7, 88

B

Babri Masjid, Ayodhya 121
Bagai, Vaisho Das 42
Bakhna, Baba Sohan Singh 27
Bal Vihar 76
Balsara, Bhicaji Franji 36
Bangladesh xi-xiii
BAPS Temple, Chino Hills 72
Barakatullah, Mahomed 25
Barbie Diwali Doll 5
Barred Zone Act of 1917 34-35, 53
Barsana Dham 75-76
Beecher, Rev. Ward 14
Bellingham, Washington 17
    racial attacks in 20-21
Bengal 23-24

Clive, Robert 3
colonialism, British ix, 8, 16-17, 23-30
Columbus ix, 75
Concord, Mass. 8, 18
Coolidge, President Calvin 68
Curry Mile, in Manchester 2

D

da Gama, Vasco ix
Das, Mary K. 40
Das, Rajani Kanta 46-47
Das, Sarangadhar 23
Das, Taraknath 27, 40, 43, 46
Dattak 132-33
Desai, Anita 3
Desai, Bhairavi 126
Desai, Kiran 3
Desai, Navin 49
desh x-xi
desis x-xi,
    (see also Indian Americans)
diaspora
    English 2-3
    Ghadr 26-30
    Global Indian 1-6, 117-18, 122
    Sikh 16-17, 118-19
    studies of 1-6
Divakaruni, Chitra 111
Dolla, Abdullah 35
dotbusters 61
D'Souza, Dinesh 125
duBois, W. E. B. 125
Dutton, Charles E. 10-11

E

East India Company 3, 8, 13
Elst, Koenrad 88
Emerson, Ralph Waldo 8-10, 37
Emerson, Rev. William 8

F

Federation of Hindu Associations 122
Federation of Indian Associations 78
Fiji 3, 4
Fisher, Maxine P. 54
Fisher, Michael 42
Franklin, Benjamin 34-35, 44
Frawley, David 88

L

Ladoo, Harold Sonny   3
Lahiri, Jhumpa   110
Lajpat Rai, Lala   25
Lanman, Charles   12
lascars   42-43
Lease Drivers Coalition   126
Leonard, Karen   44
Little Indias   123
Lockley, Fred   20
London   25-26
Los Angeles   46, 49, 62, 68-69, 73, 82, 100, 109, 122-23
Luce, Clare   50-52
Luce-Cellar Act (1946)   51

M

Malaysia   3
Maldives   xii
Maniam, K. S.   3
Mathew, Biju   126
Maugham, Somerset   2
Mazumdar, Haridas   46, 48
McCarran-Walter Act of 1952   53
Mehta, Suketu   109
Mehta, V. S.   107-08
Mexico   43-45
missionaries, view of India   8-9
Mississippi Masala   54
Mistry, Rohinton   3
Mittal, Lakshmi   3
Modi, Narendra   95-98
    campaign against, in U.S.   96-98
Mody, Navroze   61
Montesquieu   21
Mozumdar, Akhoy Kumar   36, 39
Mukerji, Dhan Gopal   46-47
Mukherjee, Bharati   110
multiculturalism   78, 94, 113-14, 116, 118, 123
Musharraf, General Pervez   123
Muslims   xiii, 30, 84, 86, 92, 95, 102, 116, 119-22
Myanmar   xii

N

Nadkarni, Subhas   71
Naipaul, Shiva   3
Naipaul, V. S.   3, 93, 107-08
Nair, Mira   54
Narayan, R. K.   107-08

Ritambara, Sadhvi   122
Rivaaj   112
Robertson, Pat   9
Roosevelt, Franklin   50
Rushdie, Salman   3, 108
Rustin, Bayard   48
Rustomjee, Customjee   14

S
SAARC   xiv
Salem   8
Samras, Khairata Ram   49
San Francisco   14-15, 21, 26-27, 32, 49, 62, 66, 78, 99, 124
Saund, Dalip Singh   51-52
Saxenian, AnnaLee   59
Self-Realization Fellowship   68
Sen, Amartya   107-08
September 9, 2001 bombings   xiii, 119
Seth, Vikram   3, 108
Sharma, Om Dutt & Krishna   100
shilpa sastras   72
Shri Lakshmi Narayan Mandir (New York)   72-73
Shri Swaminarayan Mandir (BAPS)   71
Sikh American Legal Defense & Education Fund (SALDEF)   119
Sikhs   xiii, 16-18, 76, 118-19
Silicon Valley   59-60, 86, 100, 108, 114
Singh, Gurdit   32
Singh, Jawala   41
Solanki, Uka   100
South Asia, as geopolitical area   xii, 54
South Asian Americans   x-xii, 78
     (see Indian Americans)
South Asian Lesbian & Gay Association (SALGA)   78
Southeast Asia   x, 18, 28, 29, 54, 89
Special Registration   xiii
Spivak, Gayatri Chakravorty   107
Sri Venkateswara Temple (Chicago)   71
Sri Venkateswara Temple (Penn Hills)   75
Sridharani, Krishnalal   46, 48
Sri Lanka   xii
Stanford University   88, 123
Sutherland, Justice   37-38, 43
swadeshi   x
swaraj   x

T
Tagore, Rabindranath   46
Thackeray, Bal   122

Visram, Rozina   42
Vivekananda   65-66, 89
Vivekananda Monastery, Ganges   66

W
Walden Pond   7
Ward, William   12
white, whiteness   35-38, 43-44, 57-58, 113
Whitman, Walt   10, 37
Wright, Mrs. John Henry   66

Y
Yadunandan Center (Long Beach)   100
Yagoda Satsang Society   67
Yale, Elihu   8
yoga   7, 68-69, 76
Yogananda   67-68

ABOUT THE AUTHOR

Vinay Lal was born in Delhi and raised in India, Indonesia, Japan, and the United States. He earned his B.A. from the Humanities Center at Johns Hopkins University in 1982. He received a M.A. from the same institution, also in 1982, for a thesis on Emerson and Indian Philosophy. He was awarded the Ph.D. with Distinction in 1992 from the Department of South Asian Languages and Civilizations at the University of Chicago, receiving the Marc Galler Prize for the best dissertation in the Division of the Humanities. Vinay joined the history faculty at UCLA in Fall 1993 after a short stint at Columbia University's Society of Fellows.

Vinay teaches a broad range of courses in Indian history, comparative colonial histories, subaltern history and Indian historiography and graduate seminars on the contemporary politics of knowledge, postcolonial theory, and the politics of culture. His research interests encompass, besides the subjects enumerated above, the popular and public culture of South Asia, the worldwide Indian diaspora (especially in the U.S., Fiji, Trinidad, Malaysia, and South Africa), the politics of race, religion, and ethnicity, the rise of Hindutva, the modern Indian city, the poetics and politics of water, Hindi cinema, and manifestations of the American empire.

His publications include *Empire of Knowledge: Culture and Plurality in the Global Economy* (Pluto Press, 2002; rev. and enlarged ed., Delhi: Sage, 2005); *Of Cricket, Guinness and Gandhi: Essays on Indian History and Culture* (Seagull Press, 2003; paperback ed., Penguin, 2005); *The History of History: Politics and Scholarship in Modern India* (Oxford University Press, 2003; 2nd ed., 2005); and *Introducing Hinduism* (Icon Books, 2005; translations into Korean, Spanish, and Finnish). He is the editor of *Dissenting Knowledges, Open Futures: The Multiple Selves and Strange Destinations of Ashis Nandy* (Oxford, 2000), and has co-edited with Ashis Nandy *The Future of Knowledge and Culture: A Dictionary for the Twenty-first Century* (Viking/Penguin, 2005; Kannada trans., 2007), as well as *Fingerprinting Popular Culture: The Mythic and the Iconic in Indian Cinema* (Oxford, 2006).